ADVENTURES IN FLIGHT

CONTENTS

FLYING DAREDEVILS
OF THE
ROARING TWENTIES

Plane builder Glenn Martin barnstormed the United States and Canada prior to World War I in homebuilt biplanes.

1/THEY RODE THE WILD WIND

BARNSTORMERS! It's a word to evoke a host of exciting images—of daring young men in bug-eyed goggles, caps set around backward, flying their flimsy machines through the air like erratic, colorful butterflies in high spirits, laughing at death!

Rooted in the carefree happy-go-lucky tradition of show business, the word was adopted by early aviators and made their very own . . . and so when you use it, do it affectionately, even with awe and respect, for that was the way people spoke it long before the first airliners flew, back in those dim years when man freed himself from the shackles of gravity and found a high road of adventure in the sky, that limitless arena for performing crazy stunts.

By long usage, the word now brings forth visions of wing walkers, parachutists and wild-eyed stunt fliers flashing low over county fairgrounds, scaring people half to death. True, that's the way it was in the Roaring Twenties, when the gypsy fliers spread their linen wings over the land to prove that flying was really safe after all, and not just for supermen.

But during the initial faltering steps toward the stars, when man first grew wings, when he dared to venture away from home and go chasing distant rivers, mountain ranges and far horizons, romance and adventure were part of the picture, too. At that time, barnstorming was only in swaddling clothes.

Curiously, it all began as a family affair. At first there were the brothers Lilienthal, the brothers Wright, and even the brothers Montgolfier, if one cares to go back to the first hot-air balloon days of two centuries ago. When the airplane was a *fait accompli,* a thing that really worked, the first to fly away from the nest were roving bands of barnstormers who called themselves by a different name—*exhibition fliers.*

In the year 1910, three exhibition teams held the spotlight both in the

1

Magician Harry Houdini bought Voisin biplane in Germany, took it to Australia, where he barnstormed in 1909.

United States and abroad—the Wright Exhibition Company, the Curtiss Exhibition Company and the Moisant International Fliers. Because the story of the first two teams has been told enough times to become a part of the American legend, let's take a look at the Moisants, as daring and colorful a group of aerial wanderers as ever brought shrieks of terror from gaping crowds in the grandstands at county fairs.

John B. Moisant, leader of the clan, born in Chicago in 1868, was respectable enough when he studied architecture in a San Francisco university. It even appeared that he was headed for a humdrum life as a hotel operator when he and his brothers, George and Edward, went to Central America to seek their fortunes. Similarly, his sister, Matilde, seemed destined for a career as a school teacher.

Then, on a business trip to San Salvador, the brothers found themselves

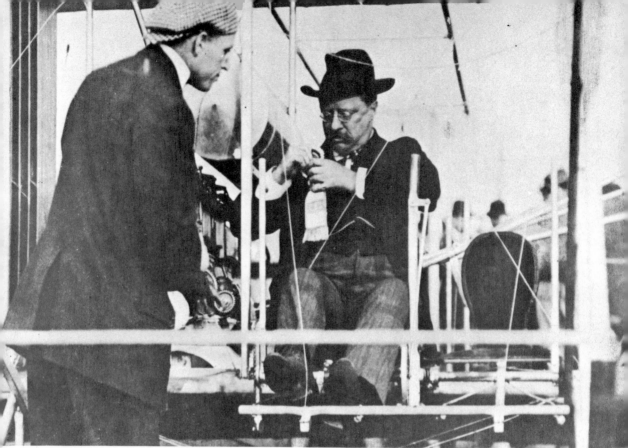

Wright Exhibition team flier Arch Hoxsey takes Teddy Roosevelt for plane ride over St. Louis in summer of 1910.

embroiled in a brewing revolution, and things began to happen fast. Their property was confiscated, and George and Edward were imprisoned. John set out for Nicaragua, alone and without funds. He didn't go to the American consulate and ask for help; instead, he angrily recruited a small army in the Nicaraguan jungle and marched back to the San Salvador border at the head of a column of three hundred armed men.

To strengthen his hand, the President of Nicaragua supplied John Moisant with an armed gunboat, the *Monotombo,* plus a hundred hand-picked men from the Nicaraguan army and two hundred native Indians who were induced to "volunteer" for the reprisal expedition. At noon, June 12, 1907, the *Monotombo* chugged into the Bay of Acajutla and opened fire on the fortress. Within minutes a white flag appeared over a parapet, and before the sun went down, Moisant had carried the day.

Curtiss Exhibition team flier Eugene Ely, first man to land on a carrier, barnstormed in Curtiss "outrigger" biplane. He died in crash on October 20, 1911, in Macon, Georgia.

With his brothers freed, John Moisant decided that business in Central America was too risky, so he sailed for France, the country of his forefathers where flying was now all the rage. Seeing a chance for new adventure, Moisant enrolled in Louis Blériot's flying school, and after three lessons he knew he had found where he belonged.

On August 24, 1910, at the controls of a brand new Blériot monoplane, John Moisant set out from Paris to establish a record by making the first international flight from one capital to another. His destination was London. Sweeping out over the English Channel, Moisant battled unexpected winds that tossed his frail aircraft about like an autumn leaf. Finally, the white cliffs of Dover passed beneath his dragonfly wings, and as he headed inland, along the Thames, people ran into the streets to wave a welcome. Moisant happily waved back. Only six miles from his destination, however, his engine began to slow down and finally stopped. He glided down to land in a small field.

Not one to give up easily, Moisant tried again and made it on September 6, winning the London *Daily Mail* Trophy for being the first to cross "the

4

Ditch" with a passenger, his mechanic, Albert Fileux. He actually had a second passenger on that historic hop—a striped cat that meowed happily for the photographers in London, glad no doubt to be back on the ground.

Air meets were now attracting large crowds in the United States, and so in October Moisant set sail for his homeland to participate in the Gordon Bennett Aviation Cup Race and International Meet at Belmont Park, New York, the first of a series of competitions he would enter under the auspices of the controlling Aero Club of America. Together with the Wright and Curtiss teams, Moisant's International Aviators held a corner on exhibition flying in those first years of barnstorming.

When Moisant returned to the United States from France, he brought with him the pick of the crop of European pilots, including such famed Gallic birdmen as René Barrier, René Simon and the great Roland Garros. Also in the Moisant troupe was an Italian pilot, Oresces Farrara, and two Americans who joined him in the United States, St. Croix Johnstone and John J. Frisbie.

With the coming of winter weather, the Moisant International Aviators headed south to barnstorm new territory. They were joined by another American pilot, Charles K. Hamilton, who had had a falling out with Glenn Curtiss. Hamilton owned a special plane, the *Hamiltonian,* powered with a 110-horsepower V-8 Christie engine. It was too hot to handle, and Hamilton had one bad smashup after another in it, frequently suffering a shower of scalding water from a broken radiator.

At Richmond, Memphis and Chattanooga, the Moisant troupe gave thousands of amazed spectators their first look at an airplane, and then they moved deeper into the South, putting on performances at Tupelo, Mississippi, and at New Orleans, Louisiana. There, as it did to many early birdmen, the way it also would to other subsequent barnstormers, sudden death came to John Moisant—wearing his flying boots.

John Moisant's death, however, did not eliminate the family name from the roster of active birdmen, or birdwomen. The following summer, his sister, Matilde, enrolled in a flying school John had started in Garden City, New York, along with a close friend, Harriet Quimby, a young and pretty drama critic of *Leslie's Weekly* who was fascinated by airplanes.

From the start, the two girls staged a friendly rivalry to see who would be the first to solo and the first female to win a pilot's license. A French instructor, André Houpert, took each girl in turn and explained all that he knew about airplanes. After thirty-three lessons adding up to four and a half hours air time, Harriet was the first to solo, on August 1, 1911.

Matilde wasn't too disappointed. On the 13th, she also ventured into the air alone. Defying superstition, Harriet promptly named her lovely Blériot monoplane *Lucky Thirteen,* for good reason: she had been born on a Friday the 13th; her first and last names began with the thirteenth letter; she applied for her flying license on the thirteenth day of the month and got it on the thirteenth of the following month!

On her twenty-fifth birthday, Matilde began her barnstorming career by following the sky trails blazed by her late brother, John. Joining the Moisant International Aviators group, she immediately set a world altitude record for women (1,500 feet!) and then traveled with the team to Mexico City to become (on November 13) the first birdgirl to fly there.

The laughing, dark-haired beauty caused gossips' tongues to wag. She was the first to wear a divided skirt, a necessity in the interest of modesty for riding in the open cockpits of her day. Harriet, not to be outdone, adopted an even more spectacular costume—trousers tucked into high-laced boots, a

America's first great exhibition flier was Lincoln Beachey, shown here taking off on flight from San Francisco, March 14, 1915, which ended in fatal crash.

long-sleeved blouse with a turtleneck and a capuchin, all made of mauve-colored satin.

Back in the United States, Matilde aroused the wrath of the constabulary of Mineola, Long Island, by breaking the "blue laws" with an exhibition flight on a Sunday. When the sheriff sent men to arrest her, she spun her ship around, dusted them good and proper, and took off again, to land at nearby Moisant Field. There other officers hauled her into court, but a Hempstead justice ruled that flying close to heaven on a Sunday was in violation of no man-made law, or heavenly one, for that matter.

Matilde and Harriet decided to team up, and for a while they barnstormed the country together. Harriet, concerned over Matilde's apparent disregard for her life, admonished, "Honey, Number Thirteen may come up once too often for you, so look out!"

Harriet herself seemed driven to take bigger and bigger risks in flying. On April 16, 1912, she was poised on the Dover cliffs of England, the nose of her frail winged moth pointed toward France. She wanted to be the first woman to cross the English Channel by air. In her exclusive report in *Leslie's Weekly,* she wrote:

"I was hardly out of sight of the cheering crowd before I hit a fog bank and found my needle of invaluable assistance. I could not see above, below or ahead. I ascended to a height of six thousand feet, hoping to escape the mist that enveloped me. It was bitter cold—the kind of cold that chills to the bones. . . . A glance at my compass reassured me that I was on my course. Failing to strike clear air, I determined to descend again.

"It was then that I came near a mishap. The machine tilted to a steep angle, causing the gasoline to flood and my engine to misfire. I figured on pancaking down so as to strike the water with the plane in a floating position. But, greatly to my relief, the gasoline quickly burned out and my engine resumed an even purr. A glance at the watch on my wrist reminded me that I should be near the French coast. Soon a gleaming strip of white sand flashed by, green grass caught my eyes, and I knew I was within my goal."

Back home once more, Harriet Quimby was hailed as a heroine of the sky. Other young women eagerly read every word she wrote. In *Good Housekeeping,* she warned girls who might take up flying that "only a

Early birdman De Lloyd Thompson, in Day biplane tractor, races speed king Barney Oldfield. The year is 1915.

cautious person should fly; I never mount my machine until every wire and screw has been tested. I have never had an accident in the air."

As every pilot knows, it's bad luck to brag about your good fortune, and when you do, you're supposed to knock on wood. But where Matilde flaunted her superstitious fetish of Number Thirteen, Harriet never trusted to luck. It was true, nevertheless, that on each flight she did wear an antique necklace over her mauve blouse and that beneath it, close to the warmth of her body, there nestled a tiny, headless brass icon given to her by a French airman (she had accidentally decapitated it one day by slamming it to the floor when everything seemed to go wrong).

But she thought it more important to leave the care of her Blériot monoplane in the hands of a competent mechanic and her barnstorming business in the care of a scrupulous manager, A. Leo Stevens. She was determined to make flying as safe as possible.

And on July 1, 1912, warming up her engine with special care at the edge of Harvard Field, Boston, there was no premonition of impending disaster. Riding with her was a passenger, William A. P. Willard, manager of the air meet, who had asked to fly with the popular girl barnstormer as a special favor.

8

Harriet was seen to smile back at him, finger her necklace for a moment, then open the throttle wide and swing her plane into the wind for takeoff.

Down the field she roared, lifting into the air as gracefully as a seagull, then spiraling upward, higher and higher, thousands of feet above the harbor. As the crowd below watched, Harriet's tiny Blériot machine suddenly nosed into a vertical dive, and an object was seen to plummet from it—the body of a man! Neither occupant wore safety belts, and whatever happened—no one is certain to this day—the sudden dive catapulted Willard from the plane to plunge through the sky, clawing at the air until he struck the water and died.

Many of the screaming, shocked spectators following Willard's body with their eyes failed to see a second form hurtle from the diving monoplane, but those who did cried out: "There goes Harriet!"

The impossible had happened; the unbelievable now was to be believed. Harriet Quimby, the darling of the skies, was mortal, after all, and flying was still the most dangerous game. Shocked most of all, of course, was Matilde Moisant, who had been in the air at the time and had seen the whole thing happen. Stealing her nerves, she immediately landed and hurried over to where rescuers had taken the bodies of the victims.

Reporters crowded around Matilde, asking for some comment. Wiping away tears, she told them, "No accident except that to my brother Jack affected me so much . . . when I think how she was always scolding me for my carelessness, and here I am after all my accidents, while she had to die in her first mishap. Well, after all, flying's like that—just a game of poker. . . ."

Harriet's death was a severe blow to Matilde, but pluckily she kept on flying her frail little Blériot, *Lucky Thirteen,* until a series of near-fatal accidents prompted her family to beg her to give up flying. At Shreveport, Louisiana, her plane's undercarriage caught on a hummock during a landing and *Lucky Thirteen* did a complete somersault, landing on top of its pilot. Still, she escaped unscathed. A few days later, at Wichita Falls, Texas, flying again proved to be "a game of poker" to Matilde when on a landing approach she saw a swarm of people suddenly sprint out onto the field, directly in her path. Reacting instinctively, she advanced the spark lever and the idling engine caught hold, but not quickly enough. She pulled up into a stall, then came crashing back to earth, the fuel tank ripping off and bursting into flames.

Those nearest to *Lucky Thirteen* grabbed a wingtip and tried to haul the blazing wreckage away, but the girl pilot was nowhere to be seen.

"Hurry!" a woman cried frantically. "She'll be cremated!"

Then, as if by a miracle, Matilde Moisant wriggled free of the pyre. Her hair was singed, but otherwise she was unharmed. It was obvious, at last, that death was hovering too close for comfort. Heeding her parents' wishes, Matilde finally hung up her helmet and goggles for good.

Ruth Bancroft Law, who had learned flying from a spectacular exhibition flyer, Lincoln Beachey, made her first public flight over Boston Harbor immediately after the death of Harriet Quimby. Until she retired from active flying in the early 1920's, her barnstorming career followed the same pattern as Matilde Moisant's, that is, as a family affair.

Ruth's brother, Rodman Law, was first to become airminded when, on February 2, 1912, he took up parachuting—by leaping from the upraised arm of the Statue of Liberty. Living through that, Law, a steeplejack by profession, made more headline jumps—from the Brooklyn Bridge, from the roof of a New York skyscraper, and finally, on April 13, 1912, from a Burgess-Wright hydroplane over Marblehead, Massachusetts.

As the second man in the world to leap from an airplane (following Captain Albert Berry, a St. Louis balloonist and parachutist) Law proved a big attraction at county fairs. Until World War I erupted, he traveled about the countryside, leaping from planes, as one of aviation's first true barnstormers.

Ruth Law barnstormed the countryside in Curtiss pusher after learning to fly under Lincoln Beachey.

Victor Carlstrom flew 462 miles nonstop to set record in 1916.

Ruth once, in August, 1914, flew her daredevil brother up to jump altitude over Salem, New Hampshire; and on December 17, 1915, anniversary of the first flight of the Wright biplane at Kitty Hawk, North Carolina, she became the first woman to loop the loop. When the country went to war, Ruth began flying Liberty Bond promotion tours; and when the Statue of Liberty was first illuminated, she circled it at night with magnesium flares blazing from her wingtips.

In November, 1916, Ruth set out from Chicago in a Curtiss pusher to attempt a nonstop flight to New York City. She ran out of gas over Hornell, New York, and landed "deadstick" at a racetrack infield, having covered 590 miles in 5 hours 45 minutes to break the former nonstop flight record of 462 miles, set earlier that year by Victor Carlstrom.

During the war, Ruth and her husband, Charles Oliver, went overseas to assess the state of flying in France, and on her return she attempted to enlist as a combat pilot. Her offer refused, she joined the American Red Cross to help out in the first Liberty Loan drive. She once buzzed the length of Pennsylvania Avenue in Washington, D.C., her wingtips grazing trees lining that thoroughfare.

The war over, Ruth and her husband sailed for the Philippines where she personally assisted in the establishment of a pioneer air route on the island of Luzon. She returned to barnstorm America for a few more years, then quit, as Matilde Moisant had done, when death seemed to be hovering too close. On October 4, 1921, at Long Branch, New Jersey, flying a ship with a rope ladder dangling over a speeding car, Ruth had been shocked to see a stunt girl, Madeline Davis, leap for the ladder and miss. Madeline struck the ground at better than 60 mph, and was killed.

Retiring to Beverly Hills, California, Ruth Law told an interviewer why

11

she gave up flying: "Things are so proper now. . . . A pilot has so many rules and regulations to follow. . . . I couldn't skim over rooftops today or land in the streets or on a race track. The good old crazy days of flying are gone."

In the "good old crazy days of flying," perhaps the best known family of barnstormers was the Stinsons—Katherine, Marjorie, Eddie and John—who hailed from Jackson, Mississippi. Katherine was barely seventeen when she went up for her first plane ride at Kinloch Field, St. Louis, with Tony Jannus, instructor at Tom Benoist's aviation school. Later, the Stinsons moved to Chicago, where Katherine acquired her pilot license on July 24, 1912, to become the world's youngest female flyer.

Not until the next spring, at Cicero Field, Chicago, did Katherine begin her career as an exhibition flier, in a brand-new Wright Model B pusher. It was the start of a barnstorming tour that would take her to Coney Island, Arkansas, Montana, Louisiana, Texas, North Dakota, Michigan and Missouri.

Her older brother, Eddie, served as Katherine's traveling companion and mechanic. In repayment she taught him to fly. Wintering at Fort Sam Houston, San Antonio, all four of the Stinsons became expert pilots and opened a flying school of their own.

When in San Francisco, in 1915, the noted stunt pilot Lincoln Beachey was killed, pulling the wings off a swift little monoplane, the *Beachey Special,* Katherine bought the wreckage, salvaged the rotary engine and had a skilled plane designer, Matty Laird, install it in a special exhibition tractor ship. With it she thrilled crowds by looping the loop and, before Ruth Law, by flying at night with flares on her wingtips.

In 1917, Katherine sailed for the Orient, barnstorming through Japan and China, then returned when the United States and Germany went to war. Like Ruth Law, she tried to enlist as a combat pilot, but her services were de-

Rodman Law gave up exhibition jumping to join Signal Corps as a balloonist in World War I.

NATIONAL AIR & SPACE MUSEUM

Aviatrix Katherine Stinson's sister, Marjorie, age seventeen, is sworn in as a mail carrier in 1914. Their mother is at extreme left.

clined. She and Marge then settled for training pilots for the Royal Canadian Air Force. With the school running smoothly, she helped the American Red Cross over the top in its Liberty Loan drive by a spectacular cross-country flight in a Jenny from Albany, New York, to Washington, D.C.

On the first leg of that flight, Katherine raced and beat the crack Empire State Express passenger train into New York City, then followed the "iron beam" into Philadelphia with a railroad timetable for a map. She finally made it to the national capital, landing beside the Washington Monument. A cheering throng of five thousand people hailed her as a real heroine when she handed a check for $2,000,000, the proceeds from her spectacular benefit aerial performances, to Secretary of the Treasury William Gibbs McAdoo.

Katherine gave up flying when she married at the age of twenty-five, while Eddie went on to become the "dean" of aviation, the first to log more than fifteen thousand hours in the air. As a plane manufacturer, Eddie Stinson built the transatlantic ship flown by Ruth Elder and George Haldeman and designed a popular line of private aircraft that is still flying.

Selling airplanes meant traveling around the country, and in that sense Eddie Stinson joined the ranks of postwar barnstormers whose air paths frequently crossed in a number of small Midwestern towns. For a time he was joined by another traveling airplane salesman, Carl Squier, who would later become the president of Lockheed Aircraft Company.

13

The Aviator—The Superman of Now

The world has its eyes on the flying man. Flying is the greatest sport of red-blooded, virile manhood.

Make your vacation the greatest you ever had by joining the Wright Flying School. Live in the open—in the aviators' tent city. Convenient hotels for the fastidious.

A short course at the Wright camp will fit you to fly any type of machine. Expert instruction in flying, assembly, upkeep, motor-overhaul, etc. Dual controls. Pupil flies the first lesson. The school is located on Hempstead Plains—the greatest aerodrome in America.

Send for New Booklet

WRIGHT FLYING FIELD, Inc.

60 Broadway, New York

By 1916 the Wright brothers had added a cockpit to their pusher planes and opened a flying school on Long Island, New York.

2/THE HERO

I WAS SIX YEARS OLD when I first met a real life birdman, gypsy flier, or barnstormer, call him what you will. I don't remember his name, but I will never forget what he looked like.

It was a warm summer day in 1919 when he buzzed our summer home at Canada Lake, New York, and with a catch in my throat I watched him finally zoom off, waggling his wings, and head for the community of Wheelerville, some five miles away.

"Daddy!" I cried. "Let's go see the airplane!"

By the time our Model T Ford was bouncing across the clover field toward the beautiful winged machine, the pilot, a tall, lanky fellow in leather coat, whipcord breeches and shining puttees, already was busy pouring gasoline from a five-gallon tin into the wing tank through a chamois skin inside a funnel.

I jumped down, raced to the airplane, and stared at it in wonder. Dad said it was a Jenny, but I thought it should have a more godlike name, for certainly the man who was up there on the wing was some kind of god.

His lean face was oil-streaked, and a trace of a smile flickered beneath a precise waxed moustache. The corners of his eyes crinkled. Goggles on his forehead made another pair of eyes against the leather helmet he wore, the ear flaps turned up.

"Here, kid!" he called, tossing me the empty gas can.

I caught it and set it down, feeling proud that I had been noticed.

"Want to go for a ride?"

My heart stopped beating. "Sure!" I cried. "Can I, Dad?"

The pilot turned to my father. "Five bucks for five minutes. And your sister can go too," he said to me.

15

Phoebe's face broke into a smile. Dwig and Betsy, our understanding parents. looked at each other, and Mother bit her lip. "Let's let them go," she finally said. "It will be a wonderful experience!"

Moments later, strapped side by side into the open front cockpit of the wonderful biplane, we were bouncing over the field and then suddenly flying! With a great leap the Jenny hurtled a fence, shot across the Wheelerville sawmill pond and began an easy, graceful climb toward Canada Lake.

Half out of the seat, I peered over the side, the wind bringing tears to my eyes and the sweet smell of burning castor oil to my nostrils. We were flying! There was nothing holding us up! Nothing but thin air, a miracle!

Phoebe's elbow nudged me. She pointed down to a bend in the shoreline. There it was—our home!

Above the hammering of the OX-5 engine I faintly heard the pilot's voice: "Sit down! You wanna fall out?"

I reluctantly slid back onto the seat cushion and then gasped as he dropped the left wing. We were going to tip over! But we didn't. Down we flew through the spiral glide, around and around as our home, the "Dwigwam," appeared pinned off the end of the wingtip, like a butterfly on a specimen board.

At once my thoughts were down there, where I liked to lie on the boathouse roof, look up at the clouds and wonder what it would be like, being a bird.

Now here I was, seeing the world from a new point of view, and marveling. I knew then what I wanted to be when I grew up—a pilot! Free to wander through the clouds and look down on the greens and browns of the countryside and follow wheeling hawks that hunted along the swampy shores of a hidden lake, the secret place of my boy's world.

Suddenly we were streaking back toward Wheelerville, the five minutes running out all too soon. I felt a sadness as we came back over the millpond and the pilot banked around, diving down toward the field where Mom and Dad stood waving beside the car.

With a jarring bump the wheels struck a clump of grass, sending the airplane careening to the left. The pilot struggled with the controls to straighten it out, but around we went in an ever-tightening spiral, until the right wing began dragging the ground.

There were no brakes on the Jenny, but if there had been, it would have been too late. We had already ripped the cloth off the wingtip. We'd ground-looped.

The Model T Ford came bouncing across the field toward us, Mother waving frantically.

"Is everything all right?" she cried as the pilot jumped down and walked toward the wingtip.

"Sure!" he replied. "I always land this way!"

He went back to his cockpit and got out a black satchel, selected a piece of canvas and a can of dope. In less than a minute he then expertly slapped the fabric over the wingtip and glued it down with the sharp-smelling stuff.

"Now," he grinned at my folks, "anybody else want to take a chance?"

He was one of an army of ex-military pilots who roamed the land with their war surplus crates, bought for $600 all boxed up, brand-new. (That's why airplanes came to be called crates, one theory has it.)

They were the gypsy fliers, out to spread the gospel of aviation to the grass roots country and to work a miracle by getting America into the air, first to wonder, then to enjoy flying, and finally to travel as a matter of course.

Airports were few and far between, but these small two-seater training planes, the JN-4D Jennies and Standards, didn't exactly need airports. Any quarter section would do, and you could tell by how green the grass was whether the field was too wet to land on, and all you needed for a wind sock was a cow's tail. Every pilot knows as well as a farmer that cows eat facing upwind.

The gypsy fliers knew it was better to land in a field near a road because then you would not have to walk so far to get gas, and if there was a barn handy, it was better to stake your airplane down behind it overnight, to keep it out of the wind.

Thus, gypsy fliers became barnstormers.

Each band of barnstormers consisted of individual heroes, for anybody who flew was obviously superior to simple ground-bound folk. They dressed the part, they lived the part—and if they swaggered a bit, they were forgiven. A country must have its heroes, and while it was fine to give special notice to generals and admirals who fought great battles, the barnstormers were of a different breed.

Facing the threat of a storm alone . . . flying into the teeth of a gale . . . winging off to remote wonderlands beyond the horizon . . . this was a new kind of stimulus, something one could understand and imagine emulating. Today one would say these were heroes "to identify with."

In the year 1919, when I met my first barnstormer and thrilled to the new world of aviation, World War I was over. The big Standard Aeroplane Factory in my home town of Plainfield, New Jersey, bulged with training planes nobody needed.

Elsewhere across the country, from Buffalo, New York, to Dayton, Ohio, and to Sy Christofferson's little Jenny factory at Palo Alto, California, thousands of war surplus biplanes posed a threat to the aircraft industry that had burgeoned.

America's air strength had been slow in growing. In the first eight years of the Army Aviation's existence, from 1909 to 1916, only 142 aircraft had been built and delivered. But the following June, Congress, facing the threat of war, made the largest single appropriation ever—$640,000,000—for a skyful of airplanes.

Flying schools mushroomed to train combat pilots for the planes we would eventually build—too late. Nearly 15,000 cadets received air training in this country and another 1,800 in Europe. By March, 1918, as the war drew toward a close, Army Aviation's strength had zoomed to 11,000 officers and 120,000 enlisted men.

Not all of these trainees were pilots, of course. At the time of the armistice, November 11, 1918, the country had at the front only 757 pilots and 481 observers, with 740 planes and 77 balloons, while another 1,402 combat-ready pilots, 769 airplanes and 252 balloon observers had entered the zone of advance.

Most of the combat planes were of foreign make, but U.S. war plants were beginning to hum at top speed, turning out copies of British designed De Havillands and Handley-Pages fitted with the American Liberty motor, our greatest technological contribution to the war in the air.

There were plenty of war aviator heroes, though. An elite of 63 Yankee flyers was credited in World War I with destroying 462 enemy planes out of the American total of 491.

These aerial killers made names for themselves that would live in history—Eddie Rickenbacker, Kiffin Yates Rockwell, Frank Luke, Didier Masson, Gervais Raoul Lufbery. They would be wined, dined and feted over and over and showered with confetti, all drawing admiring glances from pretty girls and some of them gaining fortunes.

But there were other unsung heroes who came home with only a few dollars in their pockets, a dedication to flying and no job to return to. Many were young men who had gone off to war from college and so found themselves with no career to follow. Others were country lads about whom a song had been written that asked, "How you gonna keep 'em down on the farm, after they've seen Paree?"

You couldn't. For aviation had opened a brand new world of adventure, and the taste of flying behind stinking, oil-throwing engines was still strong in their mouths. These were the men who would become the gypsy fliers.

People were optimistic at first that the Post Office Department, the Army, and the Navy could absorb the hundreds of thousands of surplus warplanes

World War I aviators, out of a job when hostilities ended, turned to barnstorming for a living.

in storage, and a glowing future was seen for sport aviation by simple conversion of the trainers.

At the beginning of 1919, one authority, Archibald Black, a Navy aeronautical engineer, wrote that "in the case of the sporting field, practically all existing types except the largest are already fairly well adapted to commercial use. The smaller and lower-powered machines, like the Curtiss JN and the Standard J, are particularly suited. The extent of this market is, of course, problematical and will depend greatly upon the large number of men of independent means who are now in the service; flying boats and seaplanes may be expected to be very popular among these men. . . ."

True, there were plenty of rich men's sons in uniform, and already one aviation enthusiast with money, Rodman Wanamaker, was organizing an Aviation Section of the New York Police Department. Wanamaker, a police commissioner, had contracted Glenn Curtiss just before the war to build a trimotor seaplane that could compete for a London *Daily Mail* $50,000 prize offered for the first transatlantic nonstop flight. Now, with the war ended, it seemed to some as though aviation would become a rich man's game.

That same year in Hollywood, California, a movie studio owner named Thomas H. Ince posted another $50,000 prize for the first transpacific flight, which was to start from his Ince Aviation Field at Venice and finish either in Australia, Japan, the Philippines or Asia.

Others in aviation took a dim view of the future of civilian flying. W. T. Thomas, president of the Thomas-Morse Aircraft Corporation, observed, "I believe there is a market for low-priced aircraft for civilian fliers, but here again, a great deal of press propaganda is needed to educate the public sufficiently to insure a sale of enough machines to allow their manufacture at a low price."

Commented Ottorino Pomilio, another airplane builder, "Unfortunately, a large number of people, and generally not through their own fault but essentially due to censorship which during the war only permitted the publication of incomplete or uninteresting news, have not yet formed an idea of what the airplane is today . . . ."

Pomilio was right. Aside from a few thrilling war dispatches about the exploits of combat airmen, to the general public an airplane was still a crazy contraption that had no practical use.

20

A few tentative steps were being taken, however, in this first year after the war. Albany, New York, established the nation's first municipal aerodrome, and the Post Office Department moved its New York "aerial mail" terminal from the Belmont Park racetrack to Newark, New Jersey, easily accessible via the Hudson tube.

There was big talk about inaugurating passenger airlines and spanning the country with air mail and cargo routes, but it was just that—big talk. The nation was caught unprepared; dreams of filling the skies with wealthy flying sportsmen and linking distant cities with scheduled airlines remained just dreams.

The frantic war economy had ground to a sudden halt. Plane factories, shipyards and munitions plants no longer swarmed with war workers. The painful aftermath of the great conflict had begun.

From the signing of the armistice to March, 1919, government aircraft contracts totaling $469,000,000 had been canceled. Searching about for some way to stimulate postwar flying, the federal ban on civilian flying, in effect through the war years, was lifted.

Flying schools rolled open their rusty corrugated metal doors for business, hopeful that the returning veterans might see a future in the sky. Among the first was the Curtiss Aviation School at Garden City, Long Island, New York, reopened under the direction of a Curtiss test pilot, Roland Rohlfs. At Tarrytown on the Hudson, the Castle School for Girls offered a course in airplane mechanics.

These were bold steps. The rich man's son, the women's rights enthusiasts, the sporting set, all found flying a fascinating new pastime, more thrilling and less expensive than yachting. But something else was needed to get people into the air, Pied Pipers who could lead the way to America's new destiny in the sky.

They finally came along, discharged Army Air Service pilots who had won a few dollars in a shipboard crap game on their way home from Europe, their worldly possessions in a duffel bag slung over their shoulders as they strode down the gangplank singing "It's a Long Way to Tipperary." They were looking forward to some kind of a career, but there just weren't any careers around. That didn't bother them, however, when they heard you could buy a brand-new flying machine for a few hundred dollars!

Almost overnight, barnstorming was born.

In tiny fields across the nation they set up shop. They didn't need to hang out shingles; everybody in town knew when they'd arrived, looping, rolling and diving overhead to draw customers out to the edge of town to buy rides. Lester Gardner, the worried editor of *Aviation* magazine, observed in October, 1919: "One of the most interesting phases of present aviation activities is the great number of small companies engaged in exhibition flights and in passenger flights of short duration. Such work has not yet reached the dignity of aerial transportation work, but nevertheless both activities have considerable educational value for the general public."

Educational? What was going on was a wild, uninhibited aviation explosion that would reshape America! The public loved it, tearing through the sky over the old folks' farm, doing loops and spirals, and buzzing girl friends' houses. It was a time for release, a time for rebirth. It was the springtime of civil aviation, and the saps were rising.

Poor Lester Gardner's voice was lost in the whirlwind when he warned, "Stunting should be avoided. Even if the passenger does ask for stunt flying, he will not enjoy it. He will come down congratulating himself on being a brave man but with the feeling he has had a very serious experience. The passenger should come down feeling that he has had a perfectly safe and normal experience which he would like to repeat . . . ."

From coast to coast they flew, these wild men of the sky, war pilots free of military discipline and enjoying immensely the role of hero.

And the public loved it. For a dollar a minute they could buy a lifetime of thrills and have something to talk about for months and years.

But there were fatalities. Through the natural course of events, the less skilled pilots killed themselves off (along with their unlucky passengers) until, by 1920, a toughened band of gypsy fliers, many of whose names are remembered today, simply took over postwar aviation.

Remember Jack Knight? Clyde Pangborn? Eddie Stinson? Frank Hawks? Art Goebel? Roscoe Turner? Carl Squier? Didier Masson? Ormer Locklear?

The list was a grease-stained honor roll of men who flew dawn to dusk, day after day, in sweaty uniforms behind overheated inline engines.

Dale Seitz . . . Frank Clarke . . . Martin Jensen . . . Boots LeBoutillier . . . these were the wood-and-wire heroes of the Roaring Twenties.

22

And there was Arrigo Balboni, the world's first flying junkman, who opened an airplane bone yard on Riverside Drive in Los Angeles and kept a famous Gold Book in his oilstreaked office, where aviation greats were glad to sign their names.

Jimmy Doolittle, Charles Lindbergh and Wiley Post were among those who stopped by Balboni's yard to pick up a used engine cowling or a wing strut, and the latest gossip.

But first you had to sign the Gold Book.

"Your name will be worth money some day," Arrigo would say glumly. "When you kill yourself."

Jennies, Standards, Canucks, De Havillands hit the barnstorming trail when the war ended.

Barnstormers got publicity by posing pretty girls with their surplus ships, like this Nieuport painted with famed death insignia of French ace Charles Nungesser.

3/FROM HAWKS TO DOVES

THEY WERE LEGENDARY FIGURES who lived legendary lives, but now the war was over and their days of glory were past, as dead as yesterday's newspaper. What would become of them, those thousands of stalwart war heroes, the gladiators of the sky? And what of the planes they flew?

After all, the war to end all wars was only a ghastly memory, and who needed warplanes with chattering machine guns? For that matter, who needed men trained to kill, men who knew no other profession than flying into the face of death?

Charles Herbert Veil, at twenty-two a veteran of the French Foreign Legion and the legendary Lafayette Flying Corps, Spad 150, *Group de Combat 16*, pocketed his *Croix de Guerre*, his *Medaille Militaire*, and his dog tags, climbed into his Spad and roared off toward Paris, anger in his heart.

He adjusted his goggles, wiped a slick of oil from his windscreen and began a long, shallow dive toward the City of Light. It was in just such a dive that he had ripped through a flight of nine Fokkers, scattering them like birds. He shot five down to win his ace rating, then hedgehopped back over the front lines, his plane riddled by bullets.

That was yesterday. Now, dead ahead, crowds filled the Champs-Élysées, cheering, crying men and women watching marching soldiers, returning heroes who had ended war forever. Veil dove down low, zipped across the Seine and threw the Spad at the columns, fingers tight on the controls. Men broke and ran. Was this fool crazy?

The Arc de Triomphe, gleaming white in the morning sun, loomed dead ahead in the crowded Place de l'Étoile. Veil made for it, his wheels inches above the crowd. At the last second he snapped over into a vertical bank and knifed through the arch, then zoomed up and slow-rolled away, grinning.

They couldn't court-martial him now! He was free to go where he wished, do as he pleased. But just in case there were any MP's around, Veil landed the Spad on a back road outside Paris, hitched a ride to the city, and boarded a train at the Gare du Nord, his destination Poland. As one of the few Americans who chose to remain abroad after the fighting, Charlie Veil barnstormed from the Bosporus to the Baltic, and in 1920 settled down at last to organize the first air line between Paris and Warsaw.

John J. Niles recalled a flying buddy named Hawkins who was bitter because a Frenchman had landed a Caudron right on the roof of the Galeries Lafayette, the big department store in the heart of Paris' shopping district. He was arrested, but he didn't mind; he had won a large bet.

Hawkins fell in love with a bridge, a lovely stone-arch bridge spanning the Seine at Choisy-le-Roi. Every afternoon for a week he flew out and looked at his bridge, swooping low to estimate the width of the span. It would be great to fly beneath it! One evening, Hawkins and Niles drove out to look it over more closely. Yes, there was enough width for his Camel, but only two-and-a-half feet of headroom to spare between the top of the arch and the water.

The next day, following a heavy rain, the skies cleared and Hawkins swung the Camel out toward Choisy-le-Roi, where Niles and other squadron mates were waiting on the bridge to see if he could make it. As Niles recalled it, the stunt ended this way:

"At the last possible moment, everything went wrong! We could almost see the whites in Hawkins' eyes as he pulled his controls back into his stomach and zoomed his plane off the river in a furious attempt to clear the bridge. His motor was going like a million. There was no reason for what had happened, as far as we could tell, except pure last-minute loss of nerve.

"As the plane shot up into the air, we had a fleeting glance at its oil-bespattered underneath. The circles of red, white and blue stood out before us like huge bull's-eyes. We had never had a chance to see the bottom of a Camel airplane up so closely—and most of us didn't care to see another under exactly the same conditions. . . . With the zoom Hawkins had pulled, considering his forward speed, the plane was thrown into an almost vertical climb. When he reached the top of the climb he began to settle a bit. Realizing this, he flattened out for an instant and tried to zoom again.

"He had cleared the bridge! But the settling movement which followed his first zoom landed him directly in front of a latticed metal telephone pole and a cross-arm strung with wires. Could he possibly raise his plane over this unforeseen obstruction or would it tip him over and land him in the river just beyond? There was a ripping sound. The metal telephone pole rocked. Jangling wires fell all about us. We dared not look up any longer. We had seen enough.

"To our great surprise, Hawkins' motor continued running. We knew he couldn't hang up there on the telephone pole forever. When we looked again, he was heading for our field. He had withstood the shock!

"Not one of us had moved. . . . Finally, we cleared out, and back at the camp we found that Hawkins had used rare judgment in landing in a seldom-used part of the field. He had brought back a unique souvenier—a dozen strands of wire tangled about his landing gear.

"After mess, Hawkins told us what had happened. As he approached the bridge he saw that there was not enough space for him to get through. We denied this—we had measured the distance the evening before! But later in the day we found our mistake—the rain had raised the stage of the river; in fact, the Seine was two feet higher than it had been the night before."

These were the ex-heroes of the First World War who turned to barnstorming . . . men seeking an outlet for pent-up emotions, trying hard to fit into a peaceful way of life. The way to do it was to buy a surplus ship and go into business, save a few dollars, and then do whatever seemed best.

Paul Baer, officially credited with destruction of nine enemy planes and unofficially with eight more, came home a hero and found the country overrun with others just like him. His Distinguished Service Cross and a nickel would buy him a cup of coffee. Nobody was interested in hearing how he had finally been shot down while trying to save a buddy or how he spent the last year of the war as a POW. Heroes were a dime a dozen.

Taking off for South America, Baer worked for a while as an airmail pilot, then drifted off to China, where he found similar employment, guiding a war surplus Curtiss amphibian in and out of Shanghai to establish a flying mail route there. For several years Baer enjoyed the life of a barnstormer in the Orient, until on December 9, 1930, he collided with a Chinese junk on the crowded Yangtze River, clipped off its mast and dove headlong back into the water. He was killed instantly.

Luckier was Lieutenant Robert S. Fogg, who had fought the war at Love Field, Dallas, Texas, as an advanced acrobatic flight instructor. Fogg spent the first three postwar years barnstorming through Texas, Oklahoma, Missouri, and Kansas, then settled down in New Hampshire to operate a seaplane service on Lake Winnipesaukee. More than thirty thousand passengers flew with Fogg without mishap, and in 1924 he was awarded the first star route R.F.D. airmail contract. Fogg became something of a legend in 1927 when the Post Office Department enlisted his aid in flying mail and emergency supplies into seriously flooded regions. For two months he flew six hundred miles a day, landing his ski-equipped plane in open fields and on mountainsides to keep the marooned inhabitants in touch with the outer world.

Earl S. Daugherty was already a veteran pilot when World War I broke out, having soloed in a Curtiss pusher at Los Angeles in 1911. Because of his experience, Daugherty was assigned as a flight instructor at North Island, San Diego, and later at March Field, near Riverside, California. After the war he joined the horde of barnstormers beating the bushes for passengers willing to take a chance on flying, five minutes for five dollars.

In July, 1921, Daugherty and another well-known barnstormer, Frank Hawks, made some kind of history with the help of an agile wing-walker named Wesley May by bringing off, the hard way, the first mid-air refueling. It was a stunt, pure and simple, dreamed up to bring out the crowds to Daugherty's small field in Long Beach, California, where he was trying to make a go of it as a fixed-base operator. By the mid-twenties, audiences already were becoming bored with routine wing-walking and parachute jumping. Some wild new stunt was needed to attract the crowds and then sell them rides. Wes May had the answer. Hawks described what happened this way:

28

Earl Daugherty and his spectacular wing-walker stunts lured customers to airport for rides.

EV HOSKING COLLECTION

"When the time came to carry out this hazardous and daring plan, a five-gallon can of gasoline was strapped on Wesley's back and I took off with him crouched on the top wing of my Standard. Daugherty already was up in his Jenny and after maneuvering long enough to build up the right amount of suspense among those watching— or rather, to give our barker on the ground a chance to build it up—we flew alongside the other ship.

"May stood up and Daugherty jockeyed his Jenny in until his lower wing was overlapping our upper one. Then the daring wing-walker, who would have been courting death under any circumstances during such a mid-air transfer from plane to plane without a parachute, but was doubly handicapped now with his awkward burden of fuel, reached up and grabbed the wing skid of Daugherty's ship, lifting himself calmly onto the other plane as I dropped down to give them leeway. Then, in full sight of the crowd and to the accompaniment of mad cheering, which none of us could hear, he walked down the length of the wing to the fuselage and poured his can of gasoline into the Jenny's regular gas tank. The first successful refueling flight in the world had been completed!"

They're all dead now—Hawks, Daugherty and May—each giving his life while following the meteoric sky trail of the barnstormer. Daugherty, who won considerable fame as a movie stunt flier, was married in an airplane, lived a full career in an airplane, and died in one on December 8, 1928, when he pulled off a wing thousands of feet over Long Beach. Hawks, who is remembered as the "Meteor Man" for his series of record-smashing speed flights above America and Europe, was killed just ten years later, when his ship flew into high-tension wires and burned. And poor Wesley May, one of the great wing-walkers and parachute jumpers, died after landing in a tree in a cemetery. He slipped from his perch and fell, fatally fracturing his head on a tombstone.

Comedy was a part of barnstorming from the start; folks not only liked to be scared to death, they enjoyed a great belly laugh, usually at somebody else's expense, boondock fliers were quick to learn. One of the favorite aerial circus clowns was William (Wild Bill) Kopia, of Newark, who began his routine by appearing at an air show when it was already half over. Dressed as a female "opera star," he would approach the box office and buy a ticket for a passenger hop. Of course, the presence of the notable performer was announced over the loudspeaker, and a ripple of applause would greet "her" as she gingerly climbed into the passenger seat of a Jenny parked in front of the grandstand with engine idling. At the last moment, the pilot would suddenly climb out and dash for the hangar to get something he had "forgotten."

The opera star, waving to the crowd, would accidentally hit the throttle and the Jenny would lurch forward, spin around, charge for the grandstand and then race off downfield in a cloud of dust. While women screamed and men yelled in excitement, the obviously petrified passenger would wave her arms helplessly. As the Jenny neared a fence, it would suddenly leap into the air and stagger back. From there on, Wild Bill Kopia put on a beautiful demonstration of skilled aerobatic flying—using a second set of controls in the front cockpit. The crowd loved it.

Not many years ago, an ex-marine named Walter O. Geary was up in a Piper Cub for his final check ride before becoming a civilian pilot, his instructor, Roland Maheu, in the front seat. As a marine, Geary naturally had lived an adventurous life, and, as far as he was concerned, Maheu was just another pilot who couldn't possibly know what real danger and excitement were. The engine suddenly stopped, and there they were, 2,500 feet up over a sea of green forest near Auburn, Maine, with no place to land.

"What'll we do?" Geary yelled.

"Get out and crank it!" Maheu grinned back at the Marine.

"I'm serious!" Geary retorted. His flight test forgotten, he was visualizing what would happen when the Cub came down in the midst of a clump of pines.

"Well," Maheu replied, "so am I!"

As the marine watched in amazement, Maheu unfastened his safety belt, flipped the door open and swung out, balancing on the landing gear and holding onto the wing strut with one hand. Then with the other he reached forward and gripped the propeller blade from behind.

"Contact!" he yelled.

Geary turned on the ignition switch, Maheu snapped down on the prop and in a moment it was purring in a steady rhythm. Maheu climbed back in-

31

Roland Maheu was capable of incredible aeronautic feats. Once when his engine stopped in midflight, he stepped out onto wing strut and pulled prop through while his copilot made contact.

side, and after admonishing his student pilot to be sure to use carburetor heat next time he started a glide on a humid day, to prevent icing, they flew back to the airport and landed.

As shocking as the stunt appeared, it was old stuff to Maheu, who had been doing it for years as a barnstorming act. Only once did he find himself in a tight spot, and that was when the propeller came to rest in a vertical position, out of reach. By turning over and reaching his leg out as far as he could, he caught the top blade with his foot and pulled it through until the engine came to life.

The Post Office Department was out of its mind, pilots said back in 1918, when the beginnings of a transcontinental airmail service were proposed to include a night run over the dangerous Allegheny Mountains from New York to Cleveland. Called the "Hell Stretch," it was a region of wild turbulence,

32

blinding fogs and hard-core clouds that concealed mountain peaks at their centers.

The ink was barely dry on the armistice agreement when the forward-looking Otto Praeger, a postal official, picked the worst day of the year, December 12, to attempt to inaugurate mail flights over the dreaded run. Not a single plane got through, nor did they make it on the second attempt on January 2, 1919. Snow squalls blinded the pilots of the Standard JR1B's, and their Hisso engines were unequal to the task of battling the elements. Angered that so much was expected of them, the airmail pilots staged history's first airmen's strike.

When some sort of scheduled mail service between New York and Chicago began later in the spring of 1919, the Post Office Department eagerly turned its eyes westward, dreaming of the day when transcontinental airmail would revolutionize the service. They had the planes—surplus Jennies, Standards, and De Havillands—but from the start they were handicapped by a lack of competent pilots. The Army was using the airmail runs to train its own birdmen.

What they needed was a special breed of airman—rugged, weather-toughened, versatile, adaptable, and with plenty of guts—someone who could find his way through a blinding snowstorm and land in a hayfield in the middle of the night with only a bonfire to guide him. Looking about, they discovered their man in the barnstormer.

Back from the wars, unemployed, beating the back country to eke out an existence hopping passengers at county fairs, these aviators fitted in with the Post Office Department credo, "The mail must go through!"

In order to get an airmail system started at a time when there were no beacons, no radio aids to navigation and few landing fields, they needed a man with more courage than brains. A smart pilot wouldn't fly under those conditions for a million dollars! But the barnstormer not only needed work, he had proven himself capable merely by staying alive at his profession and not starving to death.

With unbelievable audacity, during the closing days of President Woodrow Wilson's administration, airmail officials tried a desperate experiment to keep their service alive—a night mail run over the transcontinental route. What they needed next were men to hurdle the mountains!

33

Amazingly enough, the nerve-center of such an operation, an accurate terminal weather forecast system, simply didn't exist. In 1919, true, the Air Service had offered gypsy fliers what weather aid they could with thirty-hour forecasts of questionable value; these were issued "without assuming any responsibility for accuracy." In fact, they pleaded: "Aviators making a flight following a prediction of the meteorological officer are requested to advise him as soon as possible of the accuracy of the report"! If they were right with their guesses, fine. If not, well, it was back to the weather maps. . . .

The roster of the early airmail barnstormers is filled with heroes, the best known, of course, being Charles A. (Daredevil) Lindbergh. There were Gil Budwig, Christopher V. Pickup, Walt Shaffer and Jimmy James, to name a few. And there was Jack Knight.

In the cockpit of his De Havilland mail plane, Knight carried a notebook he'd put together during a brief barnstorming career that took him into practically every small town landing field east of the Mississippi. In the notebook were hand-drawn sketches showing the best places to land and the telephone numbers of farmers along the routes he usually followed. By phoning ahead before taking off on a cross-country flight, he had a better picture of the weather situation than he could get from official Air Service forecasts.

Flying without the aid of blind-flying instruments, it was simply a matter of luck to go up on top of the weather and hope to get back down in one piece. A couple of times Lindbergh decided the best way back was by parachute, but such a system didn't inspire much public confidence in the airmail service. Knight preferred to sneak along under the weather, following a winding road through a canyon or buzzing along the "iron beam" of a railroad track to get to where he was going. A Rand McNally road map was helpful, but in a pinch there was nothing like familiar landmarks, and Knight knew the rooftops of eastern America like the back of his hand.

On one run from Chicago to Bellefonte, Pennsylvania, Knight managed to cruise along the highways under a low-lying fogbank, then follow a powerline east until he hit the Allegheny foothills. There was nothing to do but land, or else climb on top and hope for a hole to sneak through up ahead. After a couple of hours of skimming his wheels over the cloud tops, Knight had to make a decision—jump or try to land his ship, almost out of gas.

34

Some of the early barnstormers flew the mail with a cigar as their only instrument of navigation: when they'd used up two inches it was time to land. But Knight was more scientific: he simply set his throttle for an easy letdown and took hands and feet off the controls, letting the ship descend on its own. It worked well unless he encountered rough air, which was likely to throw him into a "graveyard spiral"—and that's what happened over Bellefonte.

Groping his way down through the white mists, he knew that mountain peaks jutted up more than a thousand feet higher than the airport he sought. And in the swirling air currents, his DH, given its head, began to wander around in circles. Knight's compass spun crazily, and the wind whistling through the flying wires began to moan like keening mourners. Gingerly he pulled back on the stick, but that only made the ship dive faster. He was in a tight spiral dive! Fighting disorientation, which made everything seem upside down, he closed the throttle and jiggled the stick some more. He suddenly broke out beneath the cloud deck, plunging earthward in a sickening dive. He righted the ship just above a narrow road winding through a canyon, the mountains rising high into the clouds on either side. In relief he followed this path into Bellefonte.

Knight figured the gods were with him on that trip; in fact, he had written his last will and testament on the flyleaf of his notebook before coming down. It was this same Jack Knight who would make aviation history by carrying the night mails east from North Platte to Omaha, Nebraska, and on to Chicago on February 22, 1921, to help inaugurate the first transcontinental airmail service. Following bonfires for beacons across the lonely prairie country through the black night, he was one of a relay of pilots who performed the feat in the tradition of the old pony express. Four pilots had started off in the morning, two from New York, two from San Francisco. Both westbound planes were forced down, and the pilot of one of the eastbound ships crashed and died in Nevada. But Jack Knight, who had learned his lessons barnstorming, flew both his run and that of the Omaha pilot who was grounded in Chicago. Two other pilots completed the trip from Chicago to New York, setting a new record for transcontinental mail—33 hours 20 minutes. Through barnstorming, men trained to be hawks had proved worthy of the task of flying like doves.

35

Shades of yesterday! Rebuilt Jenny flies over Los Angeles freeway.

4/THE GYPSY FLIERS

ONE OF AVIATION's most exclusive organizations today is a group of old-time pilots who call themselves Quiet Birdmen, a fraternity that had its beginnings early in 1919 when some five hundred ex-World War I pilots banded together in New York with the express purpose of keeping flying alive.

Airplane factory shutdowns and deactivation of scores of military training fields had threatened to bring the aviation industry to a standstill just when it should have been launching itself on a great era of expansion.

At the time, inasmuch as it was generally conceded that wealthy sportsmen and returning war heroes would comprise the bulk of America's pilot fraternity, the QB's were the first to organize on that concept.

It got under way originally as the American Flying Club, and it was born in France on Armistice Day, with five hundred combat pilots for charter members. Its initial clubhouse was an old mansion off Fifth Avenue on 38th Street in New York City.

Opening in a blaze of publicity, the club tossed a gigantic party well attended by those listed in New York's social register, and a champagne dinner for members of the 94th Aero Squadron, which included such aces as Eddie Rickenbacker, Reed Chambers, Doug Campbell, Thorn Taylor, Weir Cook and Jimmie Meissner.

Handling publicity for the club was Captain Harry Bruno, who represented the Manufacturers Aircraft Association, a business organization dedicated to getting people talking about flying and overcoming their fear of getting off the ground.

The club closed its doors not long after its opening, but after that some of the members began meeting once a week at a Washington Place Italian restaurant called Marta's. There a few believers met who held to the illusion that aviation was destined for a bright civilian future—Jimmy Doolittle, Fiorello La Guardia, Clyde Pangborn, Cy Caldwell, "Pop" Cleveland, Jimmy Haizlip and others.

Bruno arranged for Casey Jones to give a plane ride to the editor of *Ace High* magazine, Harold Hersey, who had never been off the ground. Impressed, Hersey dedicated the next issue of his magazine to "the brave quiet birdmen who are patiently working in these pioneer days of aviation toward the definite goal of commercial flying."

Today, the QB's are something of a power in aviation, their secret meetings restricted to pilots only. But in 1919, they were preoccupied by the nagging question of what to do about the warehouses full of surplus warplanes that threatened to glut the market.

Bruno, working desperately for both the QB's and the Manufacturers Aircraft Association, surveyed the problem and was shocked. Nearly a billion dollars had been appropriated to darken the skies with American-built warplanes, and yet only 196 had gotten to the front and none into combat. Where had all the money gone?

There were plenty of fine aeronautical engineers and designers in the United States, and yet about the only innovation we had come up with was the Liberty engine, installed in foreign-designed craft like the De Havilland-4. A Congressional investigation was ordered, but proved little.

The upshot of this situation was that the warehouses were glutted not with combat ships but with trainers, trainers, and more trainers, mostly JN-4D Jennies, Standards and Thomas-Morse Scouts. A worried Congress, beset by aviation industry lobbyists, finally passed a law ordering the Army and Navy to unload some of their surplus planes as salvage. To the dismay of returned war pilots, these craft were ordered smashed and sold as scrap, by the pound, to keep them off the market.

In his biography, *Wings Over America,* Captain Bruno tells of being present at an army air base in 1920, "when a soldier, acting on orders, crashed a sledge hammer into the vitals of a Hispano-Suiza engine in a wartime DH-4. The sight saddened me beyond words."

A major standing beside him, William B. Robertson, also could not stand to see the lovely ships disposed of in so callous a fashion and decided to buy up the wrecks and salvage what he could. Thus was born the Robertson Aircraft Corporation in St. Louis, where Major Robertson managed to assemble from the junk pile a fleet of 225 Standard J-1's, 165 Hispano-Suiza and Curtiss-motored Jennies and 75 Liberty-motored DH-4's. With these ships he opened a flying school, and for chief pilot and instructor he hired a slender, tow-headed youth, Charles Augustus Lindbergh.

Another concerned party, alarmed at the prospect of war trainers flooding the airplane market, was the Curtiss Aeroplane & Motor Company. Opening negotiations to buy back its own products from the government, a Curtiss spokesman explained, "To sell them without guarantee among unknown buyers would be to reap a harvest of accidents and retard the development of flying."

What he meant to say was that the Curtiss factory would have to shut

Clyde Pangborn (left), a founder of Gates Flying Circus, and Colonel Roscoe Turner were charter members of QB (Quiet Birdmen) Club.

Wartime JN-4D trainer was most famed barnstormer ship. Here, with warning flag on rudder, Army cadet makes first solo.

down and scrap all its plans to enter commercial production of sport and mail planes, and so, backed against the wall, there appeared to be only one way out. Curtiss negotiated a deal to buy 2,176 Jennies and 4,608 OX-5 motors for $2,700,000. Reconditioned, these were placed on the market for what they would bring, sometimes as low as $300 each.

Down in Houston, Texas, early in 1922, a young man named Benjamin Odell "Benny" Howard heard about the Curtiss deal and applied at the company's warehouse there for a job assembling ships. Fascinated with the beautiful wood and wire wonders, Benny paid ten dollars down on a Standard biplane, looked up a man who claimed to be a pilot, and after three trips into the sky made his first solo hop.

The wind in his face and the smell of castor oil in his nostrils were a heady combination to Benny, but getting around the sky and back to earth in one piece was more a matter of luck than skill; his instructor also had only just recently soloed for the first time, and left it up to Benny to figure things out for himself.

Experimenting, Benny found that when he pulled the nose up, the singing of the wires changed pitch, and that meant it was time to put the nose down.

The technique was rudimentary, but it seemed to work fine, until one day, to pay for a needed tank of gas, he took up his first passenger, who wanted some stunts.

With his unsuspecting passenger in the front cockpit, Benny staggered up into the sky as high as he could get, which was about 1,500 feet, and there attempted his first "stunt"—a steep turn. Around and around they went, until the wires began screaming in protest. To correct things, he simply hauled back on the stick to make the nose come back up where it belonged and stop that banshee scream. Of course, all that that did was to tighten the turn and force the DH-4 into a sickening spiral.

The deadly dive continued, Benny pulling the stick back for dear life, exactly the wrong thing to do. The green earth was a blur, until finally they smacked into it with a splintering crash. Benny went to the hospital and his passenger to the morgue, but some time later Benny was up and around, walking with a limp that proved to be permanent.

Instead of being discouraged, he bought another surplus ship, sold it, and went barnstorming with the customer who bought it from him. They made it together all the way to Roanoke, Virginia, and there Benny decided he had found his career.

Having learned how to get out of a spin, Benny turned to designing airplanes and whipped up a backyard wonder that got up into the air and hit 100 mph with a 90-horsepower OX-5, a good thirty per cent faster than the Jennies and Standards flew. At eighteen, Benny, now a pilot, designer and builder of a plane that flew well, discovered that money could be made with his ideas. He sold the home-built model for $1,000, twice as much as surplus crates were bringing, then contracted to put together a kind of cargo plane for a Texas bootlegger to run whiskey across the border from Mexico.

Benny's first home-built was called the DGA-1, and the second, DGA-2. When asked what the initials meant, he replied, "Damned Good Airplane, what else?"

After a stint with the Alexander Aircraft Company in Denver as a $200-a-month "research engineer," Benny joined Major Robertson's airmail line in St. Louis, flew Ford Trimotors on the St. Louis to Chicago run before one day walking across the field and joining Transcontinental Air Transport, which had offered him more money.

After that Benny Howard found his niche building racing planes. DGA-3 was a hot little job that streaked across the sky at close to 200 mph with only a 90-horsepower Wright Gypsy engine. Called "Pete," it swept the field at the 1930 National Air Races, winning five "firsts" and two "thirds" under Benny's now-skillful piloting. DGA-4 and DGA-5 were twin racers called "Mike" and "Ike," which he flew barefooted with such breathtaking skill in closed circuit races that he was ever after known as Benny the Pylon Polisher.

With his next design, DGA-6, Benny built an amazing, four-place, high-wing monoplane with a wing-loading double that was accepted for land planes in 1933. Called *Mister Mulligan,* it was clocked at an amazing 287 mph at sea level under full 830-horsepower.

Entered in the 1935 Bendix Air Race, *Mister Mulligan* was a sleeper. The favorite to win was a souped-up Wedell-Williams Racer flown by Colonel Roscoe Turner, another barnstormer turned speed pilot, but when the two ships flashed across the finish line at Cleveland, the timers checked and double-checked their stopwatches. Vincent Bendix, the race sponsor, finally went to the microphone and announced, "The winner, by twenty-three seconds, is Benny Howard!"

DGA-6 eventually went to war as a production model designated DGA-8, her clean lines adapted to a whole line of liaison transports, secondary trainers and observation ships. Benny himself went to war in 1939 as director of flight tests for Douglas Aircraft Company's DC-4, a 240-mph cargo and troop carrier.

Another colorful QB who joined the ranks of the gypsy fliers, Captain Basil Lee Rowe, enlisted with the U.S. Army Air Service in World War I as an engine mechanic with the 871st Aero Squadron. Following his discharge, Captain Rowe bought a surplus Jenny and went barnstorming along the eastern seaboard, blazing sky trails that would be followed by scores of other itinerant pilots.

A typical back country flier who loved his work, Captain Rowe, a native of Shadaken, New York, dressed the part of the daring aviator and sported a thick mustache that gave him a look of dashing carelessness. It was only a pose; Captain Rowe was a careful, studious fellow who had big ideas about the future of flying.

In his book, *Under My Wings,* he wrote of this early period, "Flying haphazardly around the country, I developed a system of picking the profitable place to land. To test a town for its interest in flying, I would buzz it a couple of times. If the people continued about their business, I did the same. But if the animals and fowl took off for the woods and the kids tried to follow me, it indicated virgin territory. In that case I looked for a farmer's field from which to operate and, when I found one, buzzed the town to get the whole population following me out to the field like the children of Hamelin following the Pied Piper. The farmer usually let me use his field for a free ride for himself and his family.

"I would rope off my loading and unloading area to keep the people out of the propeller. I'd pick a couple of helpers from the crowd, offering them a free ride for their services. To refuel, I would walk into town with my cans and get them filled up at a gas station. We used the same fuel as automobiles. I carried my personal belongings in an old suitcase up in the front seat of the plane along with spare parts. I slept under the wing of the plane or sometimes in the farmer's barn."

After barnstorming by land from 1920 to 1926, Captain Rowe began exploring the West Indies, and for the next three years kept busy establishing a mail and passenger service that became the West Indies Aerial Express. Later on he joined Pan American Airways in Miami as chief pilot.

As an island barnstormer, Rowe lived through many unforgettable experiences. One of the most harrowing occurred during a night spent on the shore of Lake Enriquillo, after an emergency landing with his Waco on a flight from Puerto Plata to Port-au-Prince, Haiti, in 1930. He described the incident this way:

"I was over the middle of the lake when my engine began to labor and slow down. . . . I cut off the throttle and began to search the lake shore for a suitable place to set down. Logs littered the shoreline. . . . I was down to about a thousand feet when the engine started to hammer and bang."

Rowe continued on down, but just before landing he saw one of the logs suddenly scamper off; the logs were crocodiles! Rolling to a stop, Rowe leaped from the cockpit and lay on the wing long enough to make sure there were no crocodiles under him, then got busy and removed the engine's crankcase. A bearing had burned out.

He had forgotten to take along any emergency rations or water, and under the hot sun began to feel pangs of hunger and thirst. He set about gathering leaves to make a fire and boil some of the foul lake water, but then he remembered he didn't have any matches with him. Resourcefully he thought of the engine's magneto and stripped it off. Turning it by hand, he managed to create a spark that lit the leaves. He soon had a can of water boiling.

Night was falling, and he heard in the distance the frantic barking of the wild dogs of Haiti, vicious beasts descended from animals brought over from Spain by slave-runners. He rigged a tarpaulin shelter, climbed back into the cockpit with a stout stick and settled down to wait for dawn, wondering what he should do then. Something bumped his airplane. In alarm, he grabbed the stick and sat up.

"A big fight started below me in the night—great-jawed, savage crocodiles versus fanged, hungry dogs. . . . With every lurch I almost stopped breathing. With only a linen cloth separating me from what was down there, I also did a little serious praying."

The gutteral roar of the bull crocodiles and the hysterical barking of the wild dogs gave Rowe a sleepless night, but finally dawn broke, and as it did, there was a loud explosion. Rowe jumped up, then groaned. One of the tires, slashed by sharp crocodile teeth, had blown.

Wondering what to do about the bearing, Rowe stared at his feet, kicking the sand. An idea came to him: why not use the heel of his shoe? He got busy with his jackknife fashioning a bearing liner, reassembled the engine and removed the good tire to keep the Waco from ground-looping on takeoff.

Within minutes, after a precarious takeoff, he was flying again and heading for his home field at Barabona. When he arrived, his partner, Bill Wade, looked at his heelless shoe and inquired, "What happened to you?"

"I ate it," Rowe grinned.

From his barnstorming days, Captain Rowe picked up many tricks of flying that can only come from experience. In testing a new Pan Am Sikorsky S-40 Clipper on a flight from Kingston, Jamaica, to Cristóbal, Canal Zone, he used a unique application of Breguet's Law, a flight formula that says an airplane's range depends upon its flight efficiency and the ratio of fuel weight to gross weight at takeoff. This meant the lower the takeoff weight, the farther a plane could fly.

"I stripped the ship of every available ounce so I could carry extra fuel," Captain Rowe recalled. "Each reduction of six pounds meant an additional gallon, which was equivalent to two more miles. I stripped the cabin of everything, including the floor. I even sawed off the handle of my toothbrush, cut my shaving stick in half and made strip charts of my maps to save the weight of paper."

Government regulation of barnstorming was non-existent until the Air Commerce Act of 1926 placed licensing of pilots and aircraft under federal control. In 1919, the only way to stop a foolhardy gypsy flier from endangering people on the ground was to let him go kill himself first.

On January 1, 1919, Associate Editor Ladislas D'Arcy of *Aviation and Aeronautical Engineering* magazine warned that "the attitude of the Government during the war has prevented all commercial flying. The issuance of individual licenses should be commenced at once and the freest encouragement

Captain Basil Rowe (right), who barnstormed West Indies, is shown here with Colonel Charles A. Lindbergh (center) and radioman Bert Denicke, crew on first Pan American Sikorsky S-38 hop from Havana to Mia Cristobal.

Canuck was Canadian-built version of the famed Jenny.

given to all who desire to enter the aeronautical field as sportsmen or to those seeking an industrial opportunity."

As it was, anyone with a few dollars in his pockets could go buy a surplus Jenny, climb in and fly it off to operate from some cow pasture. True, barnstorming was financially a risky venture to begin with, and in the words of one ex-military aviator, Dick Depew, "the most dangerous thing about flying is the risk of starving to death!"

Even so, hordes of daring young men were lured by the prospect of owning their own airplanes and going into business for themselves, a sort of rebellion against society's regimentation, a rebellion dating back to their years in Army uniform. Wasn't it better to fly the open sky in weather-beaten ships, hopping from town to town, following the county fair circuits than to fly a desk in some dull office?

There were plenty of customers in the early days, men and women who would step forward from the crowd and heroically hand over ten dollars for ten minutes in the sky. Unforgettable was the thrill of being strapped into the front seat of a moth-like biplane, stomach knotting at the expectation of what was to come, staring at the frightening panel of dials and gadgets, hearing the ear-splitting thunder of the engine roaring to life and feeling the hot blast of exhaust fumes on your face.

There was the prideful wave of assurance to a friend waiting to watch you take off—and probably crash—a weak grin of bravado, and then the sensation of gathering speed as the frail biplane bounced along over the grassy field, leaped a fence and was *flying!*

A look back at the pilot's face, hidden beneath a tight leather helmet and goggles, brought a wave of confidence in this superman in the back seat who held your life in his hands. Then came the gradual release of tensions as you dared to look over the side and see the beauty of the world spread out below—patterns of farms, rock fences and orchards, and over there, the .schoolhouse! You forgot your fears and in the supreme enjoyment of the new experience you were getting far more than your ten dollars' worth. You were introduced to a whole new world, the world of the barnstormer.

Back on earth, you shook hands with your pilot, who casually lit a cigarette and looked over the crowd for more customers. He was a rakish sort of devil, one who seemed always to be leaning into the wind, squinting at far horizons, smelling the air for stormy weather. He was a hero.

Then there were the wing-walkers, the parachute jumpers, the aerial stuntmen who teamed up with barnstorming pilots to help gather crowds by cheating death while clambering over the outside of the fabric planes as they swooped low over towns. One such youth was described by a small-town social worker, Olga Edith Gunkle, in an article she wrote for *Scribner's Magazine* in 1929. He had come to her office to discuss giving a benefit performance to help him get his nerve back after watching a pal fall to his death from an airplane's wing:

> I had finished a list of names for him, but I still kept my pencil on it. I was rather reluctant to let this blue-eyed youth go. He was such a contrast to the battered and bescarred bits of human wreckage who came asking meal-tickets and lodgings. He made me think of limitless expanses of sky—flying clouds—wind-swept spaces—youth indomitable.
>
> "Ever see anyone hurt except your pal?"
>
> "Lots of them. One guy stumbled and fell and got the top of his head chopped by the propeller. An' then one kid—aw, you don't like to hear about it, do you? But you see you don't mind it quite so bad after a while, except when it's your pal."
>
> "Ever get hurt yourself?"
>
> "Once in a while."
>
> "Badly?"
>
> "Last time I got hurt, something went wrong with the plane and they had to land before I could climb back up the rope. I got dragged. Was unconscious for three days."

"My gracious, I'm glad I don't have to watch anything like that. I'd hate to see anyone hurt."

"Oh, you'd get used to it," he gravely remarked.

"Don't the crowds that watch you make you nervous?"

"No, ma'am. You never even think of them. You see, it's like fighting a hundred-mile gale up there, with the wind blowing and the plane moving along. You've got to spend all your time hanging on, and it sure takes every muscle in your body."

As he spoke, he gripped in imagination a wiry bit of rope and I saw the muscles in his hands and neck tense and swell. His whole body was fighting the hundred-mile gale. The musty volumes in my office faded away and I was one of the spectators staring upward with bated breath, while far up in the air a tiny figure swaved and twisted and clung to a bit of flying rope; only I was one of the spectators who knew just how young and **strong** he was, with his curly hair and gallant blue eyes. And I was fearful—horribly fearful —lest he too lose his grip and come crashing, crashing, downward. It would be such a pity! Something fine and splendid would be gone from out of the world.

Wichita, Kansas, a city destined to become famous as the "Air Capital of the World," was the launching place for Sidney Q. Noel's barnstorming career, one day in June, 1919, when he walked down the street and spied a gorgeous Curtiss JN-4 Jenny displayed in an automobile parking lot next to the Arnold Brothers Motor Company.

Noel and a buddy, James A. Ellison, just returned home from duty overseas, fell in love with the Jenny at first sight and decided then and there to buy her. That was fine with Mr. Arnold, who had purchased a pair of ships from the Curtiss factory as an investment.

"How much for that airplane?" Noel asked, kicking the tires.

Arnold sized up his customer and knew, from the light in his eyes, he had a pigeon. It was quite obvious that Noel had already made up his mind.

"Three thousand dollars and she's all yours."

"Three thousand—?" Noel cried.

When Arnold turned and started back to his office, he felt the expected tug at his sleeve. "Okay, it's a deal," Noel said. He had to have that Jenny!

Noel was no novice; he had learned to fly in the Army and completed one hundred missions over enemy lines with the 148th, a scouting squadron, and later trained on French Spads before the armistice ended his military aviation career. By then he was sold on flying.

So it was that Noel and Ellison climbed into the two cockpits one bright morning and headed south on their barnstorming adventure through Kansas, Texas and Oklahoma. Noel recalls, "We would circle a town, and by the time we landed, mostly in stubble fields, the whole town would be there. We didn't have to ask them. They came up and asked us for rides."

There was no need for wild stunt flying. The towns Noel and Ellison flew into had never seen an airplane before, with the exception of one or two when early Curtiss and Wright pushers visited back in the prewar Early Bird days.

By Christmas, 1919, the barnstormers had made enough to recoup the $3000 they had invested, and Noel bought out his partner. The next spring Noel teamed up with two other gypsy fliers to form the Salina (Kansas) Airplane Company, one of the first "flying circus" teams to barnstorm the Midwest.

While the exploits of the Salina Airplane Company were not particularly death-defying, they were representative of the growing wave of gypsy fliers who were spreading the gospel of aviation across the land, getting people used to flying in airplanes instead of looking upon them as instruments of death and destruction, an image that dated back to prewar years when bird-men like Linc Beachey, Arch Hoxsey and Hubert Latham created the legend that it takes a superman to fly.

Fred Kelly (right) opened up Cuba to flying in 1920 with a JN-4D Jenny. Later he flew for Western Air Express with Jimmy James (left). Man in middle is Herbert Hoover Jr.

WESTERN AIRLINES COLLECTION

There was, of course, another kind of gypsy flier who seemed to fly with suicidal purpose, men like Captain Frank T. Dunn, ballyhooed as "the only flier who has successfully looped the bridge of a navigable stream." Basil Rowe went Dunn one better by having a screaming blonde beauty in the front seat while diving down beneath the Philadelphia-Camden Bridge and pulling up and around in a complete loop.

The girls, naturally, went for the gypsy fliers in a big way, and the fliers in turn tried hard to live up to the heroic image of the returned war veteran who had killed enough enemy pilots to rate as an ace. While few of the early barnstormers had actually earned that status, it was only necessary to dress the part. Many held a superstitious attachment to a favorite piece of clothing. Clyde Pangborn refused to fly without his soft chamois vest, and the great Casey Jones insisted on wearing a loud green jacket. Others made sure some kind of icon dangled in their cockpits to get them safely back to earth.

If most of these early fliers placed a large amount of faith in sheer luck, there were a few who went about their work with what they believed was a "scientific" approach. One Texas barnstormer known as Crazy John flew regularly between El Paso and Dallas, and to keep from getting lost he stuck two arrows on his compass, one reading, "El Paso This Way" and the other, "Dallas That Way." In spite of this "science," he never got lost.

American barnstormers introduced aviation to Cuba after the war, although the United States Army Signal Corps had operated observation balloons at San Juan Hill during the Spanish American War. Perhaps the happiest barnstormer to find a paradise in that country was a former military flying instructor named Fred Warren Kelly, who left his job at Gerstner Field, near Lake Charles, Louisiana, in 1919 to seek his fortune in Cuba.

These five barnstormers started up Western Air Express: (left to right) Fred Kelly, Jimmy James, Al DeGarmo, Maurice Graham, C. C. Moseley. Graham froze to death in a snowstorm after a crash during a mail flight over Utah.

Shipping a war surplus Jenny to the island by boat, he and a Cuban friend, Rafael de Zaldo, established Cia. Airea Cubana, that country's first airline, so to speak, based in Havana. When a windstorm wrapped their only aircraft around a tree, Kelly went to the United States to bring back another JN-4D and a Curtiss Oriole, in which he taught Zaldo to fly.

For a while Kelly enjoyed himself stunting over town, shooting off night fireworks and hopping passengers in search of aerial thrills. When the novelty wore off, he and Zaldo flew their planes to the hinterlands in search of new customers who had never seen a plane before.

"We attracted a lot of attention, and the Cubans were eager to use our services," Kelly recalls. "We landed at Cardenas, Cienfuegos, Santa Clara, Ciego de Avila, Camaguey, Holguin and Guantanamo."

In December, 1920, at the edge of Santiago de Cuba, Kelly put the Jenny down in a small clearing before he was able to realize it was too small for a takeoff. The natives pitched in at his urging and by the next day had chopped down enough trees to make a decent runway. In return, he gave the mayor's pretty daughter a thrill ride.

Among Kelly's new-found friends in Cuba was another beautiful girl, Lolita Bacardi, daughter of the owner of the Bacardi rum distillery, who decided that the American *piloto*, along with his pal, Zaldo, were some kind of heroes who needed a medal. Lolita threw a huge party, complete with suckling pig and plenty of rum, then kissed both fliers on their cheeks and hung on their necks medallions on which was inscribed, *"Kelly y Zaldo—primer vuelo Havana-Santiago de Cuba*, December 31, 1920."

To repay her kindness, the barnstormers one morning flew over the Bacardi estate, looping and rolling and buzzing low to get everybody out of bed. When he saw Lolita in the patio, waving her handkerchief at him, Kelly banked over and threw out a bouquet of flowers.

Kelly ended his barnstorming in 1925 and returned to Los Angeles, where he became one of the first airmail pilots to fly the treacherous mountain route to Salt Lake City for the old Western Air Express. Not only was it tough flying, it could be rugged on the ground, too: A fellow pilot, Maury Graham, who had become a war hero by finding the Lost Battalion of the 77th Division, crashed in a snowstorm on that run in 1930 and froze to death trying to walk out.

51

America Trans Oceanic Co. opened offices in West Palm Beach, Florida, in 1919. For certain passengers it sometimes needed bigger boats than this Curtiss Seagull.

5/SAGA OF THE BIG FISH

AS FAR AS SHREWD old Orville Wright was concerned, the only thing wrong with flying was getting back onto the ground. Alone up there in the sky, a man had only the birds to contend with, but if his engine quit and the irresistable clutch of gravity grabbed him, look out!

At the beginning of 1919, with America entering her first peacetime year since the armistice, the airplane engine that wouldn't quit on a whim hadn't been invented yet—Orville knew. The mass-produced Liberties, the Curtiss OX series, the Hall-Scotts, the Duesenbergs, the Packards, all were great powerplants when they kept turning, but no wise pilot would risk his neck flying cross-country over difficult terrain where he couldn't glide down "dead stick" for an emergency landing when his engine quit, leaving him in a most uncomfortable silence, sitting there counting the rivets on wooden propeller blades that suddenly windmilled to a stop.

"To make flying perfectly safe," cautioned Orville Wright on January 1, 1919, "good landing places must be provided every ten to twelve miles." Orville figured that a pilot flying one mile high then would have a chance of gliding for six to eight miles and setting down on a good field.

Quite obviously, Orville had his head in the clouds on that idea. To build the hundreds of thousands of airports he envisioned scattered across the country was simply out of the question economically. Until the day came when engine reliability could guarantee that a plane would stay up for a reasonable length of time, pilots were going to have to trust to luck and their own skill in making forced landings.

A scattering of sport planes developed in America during the war years paid serious attention to the problem of short-field landings. Aircraft Engi-

53

neering Corporation's hot little Ace biplane could land in fifty feet, its makers claimed. Their slogan was, "The Country Road Your Airdrome."

Among the first to buy an Ace was barnstormer Eddie Stinson, but at $2,500, while "ideal for the ranch owner, the pilot of the aero mail, the sportsman, and the explorer," it couldn't compete with the war surplus market of Standards, JN-4Ds and Thomas-Morse Scouts that could be picked up for a few hundred dollars each.

Among the thousands of leftover military planes that would find their way into the ranks of the barnstormers, several dozen flying boats were put on sale by the government, a fact few people remember. Here were aircraft that needed no landing fields. Lakes, rivers, bays, and the oceans themselves provided all the room to roam a pilot could want, without worrying about a place to set down when trouble developed.

And of all the surplus flying boats purchased for civilian use, none had a more remarkable career than the *Big Fish*. Randolph Baldwin, the man who flew as her copilot and mechanic, grows ecstatic when he recalls the beauty of her sleek lines, her rugged stability, and her unique paint job. And he remembers her balky Liberty engines, this with a shrug of amusement that seems to say: "It was all great fun, but I wouldn't want to trust my life to them again!" More than once Randy Baldwin and his chief pilot, George A. Page, Jr., found themselves with one engine out whistling down through the sky to land in heavy sea swells somewhere between Florida and the Bahamas, where the pioneer "overseas" airline they flew for, America Trans Oceanic Company (A. T. O.), operated right after the war.

The *Big Fish* was a Curtiss H-16C, a twin-engine flying boat that had been purchased from the Navy by David H. McCullough, who, on February 24, 1920, began scheduled passenger operations between Miami, Florida, and Bimini, some forty-five miles east of the Florida coastline, in the Bahamas.

McCullough, in fact, was an old hand at making water landings with flying boats. On May 17, 1919, as one of the pilots of the Navy transatlantic flying boat NC-3, attempting an ocean crossing from America to Europe, he had become lost in the blinding whiteness of a deep fog bank, and was forced to land as the only way to find his bearings. Unable to take off again

54

because of high seas, McCullough and his crew performed a miracle by sailing the flying boat through a savage storm for 205 miles into the port that had been her destination—Ponta Delgada, in the Azores.

McCullough typified the postwar barnstormer—courageous, energetic, daring and adaptive. Bringing the NC boat through a fierce Atlantic storm that threatened to batter her to pieces with each crashing wave was an epic feat in itself, but it took real guts to refuse an offer from the skipper of a passenger liner, the *Harding*, to tow them into port.

"We came this far; we're going the rest of the way!" McCullough signaled. Chugging into port on two damaged engines, he rated a 21-gun salute from a shore battery. The NC-3 was every bit as big a hero as the NC-4, which alone made it across the Pond while they sat drifting.

The Curtiss H-16 *Big Fish* herself had an interesting history, being a development of the original *America* flying boat that Glenn Curtiss had built in 1914 for Rodman Wanamaker to fly the Atlantic. The *America*, christened on June 22, 1914, was launched on Lake Keuka at Hammondsport, New York, where Curtiss' airplane factory was located.

In 1914, Glenn Curtiss built flying boat America *for wealthy sportsman Rodman Wanamaker to fly the Atlantic. Craft was underpowered and crossing was never attempted.*
RANDOLPH BALDWIN COLLECTION

From the start, it was apparent that the *America's* two Curtiss OX-2 engines, of 100-horsepower each, were not strong enough to give her the speed and range necessary for the ocean hop, so a third engine was mounted atop the upper wing. Outbreak of war canceled all plans for the venture; her pilots, Navy Commander John H. Towers and Lieutenant John C. Porte of the British Royal Naval Air Force, went on active duty, and the craft was placed in storage behind the Curtiss flying boat hangar at Port Washington, New York.

Six miles from the Curtiss plant at Garden City, New York, hummed another wartime plane factory, the A. S. Heinrich Corporation, where Page and Baldwin were employed, and where they formed a lifetime friendship. "There never was another pilot like him," Baldwin says of Page today, his hero worship unconcealed.

Wartime responsibilities separated these two eager young men, Page joining Curtiss in his booming Navy flying boat business, and Baldwin moving to the Naval Aircraft Factory near Philadelphia, where he set up the metal and machine departments for production of Model MF flying boats.

Thus, following the armistice, Page and Baldwin were well versed in the lore of flying boats, Page as an engineering pilot and Baldwin as a mechanic, and they were immediately hired by McCullough to man an H-16 war surplus craft that, with a piscatorial paint job, would become the *Big Fish*. A tough, seaworthy craft, she had a ninety-five-foot wingspan and originally carried a crew of four—pilot, copilot, gunner-bombardier and a wireless-operator-gunner in a compartment behind the pilot's cockpit.

Converted for barnstorming, the craft carried two passengers up front and nine in the hull, in addition to pilot and copilot-mechanic. Her two Liberty engines were rated at 350-horsepower, but Baldwin managed with special domed pistons somehow to get 400-horsepower from each of them.

"We switched from castor oil to regular automotive oil and used the best grade of aviation gas we could get," he recalls. The boat's 235 gallons were enough to keep her in the air at 75 mph for 5½ hours nonstop—if she happened to fly that long without a breakdown. The Liberty engine, Page and Baldwin discovered, had a bad habit of chewing up her distributor shaft gears.

The *Big Fish* got her name from a giant, forty-ton whale-like fish landed

Big Fish *rests on water off Bimini.*

by a prominent angler, Captain Charles Thompson, who later became president of the Bimini Bay Rod & Gun Club, a resort whose guests often flew the American Trans Oceanic (ATO) boat from Miami on its triweekly run. The attractions of Bimini were more than just fishing and shooting; the Eighteenth Amendment had gone into effect June 30, 1919, and Bimini was a favorite spa for the thirsty.

Rumrunners, in fact, operated on a schedule almost as regular as that of the *Big Fish*, a fact that once worked in Randy Baldwin's favor during a hairy adventure that followed a routine forced landing, when the flying boat on a flight from Nassau had to land on the sea after one of the engines' distributor gears stripped. The landing itself was uneventful. Page, who was doing the flying, was skilled at water landings and set the *Big Fish* down between two swells not far from Andros Island, biggest of the seven hundred islands in the Bahamas chain.

"There were two native sponge boats nearby and one came over to us," Baldwin remembers. "It was a small boat, but we off-loaded our passengers and put them ashore."

All that afternoon they taxied the *Big Fish* on one engine until they found a sheltered cove, and the next day Page did a masterful job of threading the flying boat along a narrow waterway passage into Low Sound. For the next eleven days Baldwin camped out on Andros Island while Page searched the United States for parts, which he finally located at Fort Myer, Virginia. Randy quickly became disenchanted with the swarms of gnats that buzzed around him at night and finally moved aboard the *Big Fish* to sleep. When Page didn't return during the second week, Baldwin, worried, hitched a ride with a passing rum boat piloted by a bootlegger named Bruce. Baldwin and Page finally found each other, returned to repair the Liberty engine, and flew off once more to Florida.

In Miami, they made their headquarters at the Halcyon Hotel—there were no others of any consequence—but spent most of their time on the flying boat or on a small island owned by a squatter named Chris, who helped them haul fifty-gallon gasoline drums out from the mainland in his rowboat.

Navigating the open seas with only a wildly swinging compass was something of an art, for unlike their fellow barnstormers who operated over land, Randy and George had few landmarks—only an occasional cay or a distant island to help them get their bearings.

"We had no drift indicators, so we took along a ball of cotton and tossed some out from time to time. By looking back," Baldwin explained, "we could see if we were drifting to the right or the left of the cotton."

The only other flight instrument on board was a spirit level attached to the side of the hull, which served as a pitch indicator that told them when they were diving or climbing in bad weather, and there was plenty of that. On one trip they returned to the Florida mainland only to find the Miami shoreline hidden beneath a black squall line stretching from horizon to horizon. Over the inlet at Palm Beach, where they detoured, they were battered by a fierce gale that threw the flying boat all over the sky. Two women passengers up front thought Page was giving them some free acrobatics and yelled in glee, but Baldwin was saying his prayers.

"My God!" he yelled. "Get this thing back out over the ocean!"

Page circled low over the palm trees, which looked like so many agitated windmills under the force of the storm, then eased around to land inside the bay, the spray drenching everybody to the skin.

Another time, carrying eight passengers on a run to Nassau, George and Randy saw the sky ahead blacken with towering nimbus clouds. Page decided to set down the *Big Fish* to ride out the storm on what looked like smooth water behind a wind-lashed cay. At the last second before touchdown Page saw that the waves in all directions were breaking over jagged coral rocks.

He yelled, "Pull up! Pull up!" Both men hauled back on the controls. They lifted the *Big Fish* clear just in time to prevent her hull from being ripped wide open.

While the *Big Fish's* runs between the Florida coast and the various islands of the Bahamas were essentially barnstorming ventures, they served another historic purpose; in thrice-weekly flights between Miami and Bimini, they pioneered scheduled airline transportation in America many months before a competitive line, Aeromarine West Indies Airways, Inc., began hauling passengers from Key West to Havana, Cuba.

Aeromarine, which had flown that route since November 1, 1919, carrying airmail by single-engine flying boats, has long been mistakenly credited with starting the first "overseas passenger operation." Actually, their passenger runs did not get going on a regular schedule until October, 1920. Their ships were modified Curtiss F-5L Navy "flying cruisers," colorfully named the *Santa Maria, Nina, Pinta, Columbus, Balboa* and *Ponce de Leon*. But by the time they were in full swing, ATO and the *Big Fish* already had airlifted several hundred passengers from the United States to the British territory of Bimini on something like scheduled flights.

At a "special rate" of $25 each way, passengers could dash over to Bimini in a little more than half an hour. The *Big Fish*, "piloted by one of the best-known fliers in the world and assisted by an expert mechanic," advertised that it would leave Miami for the forty-five-mile run at two P.M. sharp on Wednesdays, Fridays and Sundays, returning at the same hour on Thursdays, Saturdays and Mondays.

Thus, while other owners of surplus Curtiss F-5L twin engine boats flew occasional charters to the Bahamas, the *Big Fish*, with Captain Page as pilot and Baldwin as copilot, was first to advertise regular runs to the British spas. It may be considered ironical, but the Volstead Act did provide a vital stimulus to the early start of scheduled airline service, for as Prohibition went into effect, all possible liquor was hastily shipped out of the country and piled on the beaches in the Bahamas in row after row of cases. Naturally,

59

those who liked a drink followed, for rumrunning had not yet become organized. On North Bimini Island, a Miami group erected a 105-room clubhouse which became not only an important fishing, gambling and drinking resort, but also served as a terminal office for ATO.

By February 23, 1921, the *Big Fish* had spread her fins further south, carrying tourists to Havana. One traveling VIP was Margaret Alphonso de Bourbon, a cousin of the King of Spain.

After two full seasons on the "Bimini booze run," as the scheduled Bahamas flights came to be called, the *Big Fish* left the lucrative island trade to her competition, forsaking the beauty of the Bahamas and the Antilles green-water hops. In the spring of 1922, she pointed herself northward, like a homesick duck, and joined the flights of migratory birds winging toward Canada to enjoy the long days of summer.

At Lake George, New York, she came to rest, after a brief stop at Port Washington, where Page turned her over to a new pilot named Johnny. Randy and Johnny operated her the rest of that summer, hopping passengers throughout upstate New York. Then, when autumn leaves began falling, it was time to return to Port Washington.

Pure of heart to the end, the *Big Fish* abstained, as she had in Florida, from joining in the lucrative bootleg business along the Canadian border, leaving that field to other barnstorming Jennies and Standards that slipped off overhead in the dark of night with their bellies painted black. Her short and honorable career came to a sad end in October, 1922, when Randy and Johnny winged down the Hudson River on her last flight from up north.

The lights of Poughkeepsie slipped by under her left wing as she pierced the darkness, flying lower and lower to stay beneath a fog bank that obscured the Tappan Zee from view. Baldwin flipped on a flashlight and held it on the compass for Johnny, then looked up just in time to see the Albany night boat looming dead ahead.

Swerving violently, they missed the steamer by inches. In leveling out to attempt an emergency landing, Johnny banged the hull on the water with bone-shaking force. Waves ripped off the false step on the bottom, leaving a gaping hole in the hull.

"We came to a stop, engines running, sitting there slowly sinking," Baldwin recalls. "I suddenly remembered we had passengers in back—a woman and two small children. I looked around. They already were knee-deep in water!"

Although furious with Johnny for wrecking the *Big Fish,* Baldwin was grateful to him for saving his life just at that moment. "I'd jumped up and started around to get the kids, forgetting about the propellers. Johnny grabbed me by the arm and pulled me back, just in time to keep me from getting my fool head cut off!"

The *Big Fish* finally came to rest floating on her wings. Randy dove overboard, braving the rough chop and swimming for shore two miles away. He encountered a passing motor launch and yelled for help. The boat stopped, reluctantly picked him up, and returned to tow the *Big Fish* ignominiously to shore. She was taken to Port Washington on a railroad flat car.

Later, Baldwin and Fred Golder, ATO's airport manager, returned with a can of gasoline and put the torch to her. Randy sadly watching her go up in flames, snapped a picture to remember her by. After that, ATO's operations went into a decline. The outfit flew a few more years with smaller boats, but already competition was strong as other gypsy fliers with a Navy background moved down to Florida to help skim off the cream of the tourist market. West Palm Beach was a favorite hangout for flying boat barnstormers, but few, in the mid-1920's, were able to duplicate the success of the *Big Fish.*

Up in flames goes the Big Fish, *her owners having sadly put the torch to her broken hull.*
RANDOLPH BALDWIN COLLECTION

The New York Times.

VOL. LXXVI...No. 25,320.   NEW YORK, SUNDAY, MAY 22, 1927.   FIVE CENTS

LINDBERGH DOES IT! TO PARIS IN 33½ HOURS;
FLIES 1,000 MILES THROUGH SNOW AND SLEET;
CHEERING FRENCH CARRY HIM OFF FIELD

COULD HAVE GONE 500 MILES FARTHER

Gasoline for at Least That Much More Flew at Times From 10 Feet to 10,000 Feet Above Water.

ATE ONLY ONE AND A HALF OF HIS FIVE SANDWICHES

Fell Asleep at Times but Quickly Awoke—Glimpses of His Adventure in Brief Interview at the Embassy.

CROWD ROARS THUNDEROUS WELCOME

Breaks Through Lines of Soldiers and Police and Surging to Plane Lifts Weary Flier from His Cockpit

AVIATORS RESCUE HIM FROM FRENZIED MOB OF 25,000

Paris Boulevards Ring With Celebration After Day and Night Watch—American Flag Is Called For and Wildly Acclaimed.

MAP OF LINDBERGH'S TRANSATLANTIC ROUTE, SHOWING THE SPEED OF HIS TRIP.

LINDBERGH'S OWN STORY TOMORROW

LEVINE ABANDONS BELLANCA FLIGHT

Venture Given Up as Designer Splits With Him—Plane Narrowly Escapes Burning.

BYRD'S CRAFT IS NAMED

CAPTAIN CHARLES A. LINDBERGH.
Who Flew Alone Across the Atlantic, New York to Paris, in Thirty-three and One-half Hours.

New York Stages Big Celebration After Hours of Anxious Waiting

LINDBERGH TRIUMPH THRILLS COOLIDGE

President Cables Praise to "Heroic Flier" and Concern for Nungesser and Coli.

CAPITAL THROBS WITH JOY

By EDWIN L. JAMES.

COURTESY N. Y. TIMES

A barnstormer makes good—the story of Lindy's great hop.

© 1927, 1955 The New York Times Company   Reprinted by permission.

6/DAREDEVIL LINDBERGH

A SLEEPY, Midwestern university town, Lincoln, Nebraska, had wide avenues lined with shade trees, and was dominated by the four-hundred-foot tower of the Nebraska State Capitol building. One day in June, 1922, as the town basked in the languor of a summer sun, the throaty Hisso engine of a slowly climbing Lincoln Standard biplane droned on far above in the sky. The craft circled with the sweeping grace of a hawk riding a thermal, its eyes scanning the grain fields below for a sign of movement that would reveal a scampering rabbit or squirrel. In the Standard's rear cockpit crouched a pilot named Erold Bahl, a slender man with his cap on backward and wearing a business suit in the manner of the late, great Lincoln Beachey. In the front cockpit was another slender young man wearing helmet and goggles. His name was Charles Augustus Lindbergh, and at twenty he was about to make his first parachute jump, the hard way.

Leveling off at jump altitude, Bahl was suddenly active, businesslike. He rocked the control stick, signaling Lindbergh that it was time. The helmeted youth up front waved, then unbuckled his safety belt, gripped the center wing strut and stepped out of the cockpit onto the narrow catwalk along the fuselage. He smiled at Bahl, then, remembering his instructions, made his way carefully along the wing spar, keeping his balance by holding onto the maze of flying and landing wires that criss-crossed from top wing to bottom.

He paused to steady himself, feeling the slipstream tearing at his clothing and filling his mouth with ram air. A misstep now could mean death, for his parachute lay out there near the outer bay strut, clipped to the flying wires, waiting for him to reach it and clip it to himself.

63

Far below the Standard, a small group of people stood at the edge of Lincoln Field: Ray Page, the president of Nebraska Aircraft Corporation, Bud Gurney, a close friend, Charley Harden, the man who had rigged his parachutes for him. Yes, there were two parachutes, and Lindbergh intended to use them both.

He had watched Harden make a dangerous double drop only a few days before, and it had become a compulsion to do the same. He would later write, in *The Spirit of St. Louis:* ". . . When I decided that I too must pass through the experience of a parachute jump, life rose to a higher level, to a sort of exhilarated calmness. The thought of crawling out onto the wing, through a hurricane of wind, clinging on to struts and wires hundreds of feet above the earth . . . left in me a feeling of anticipation mixed with dread, of confidence restrained by caution, of courage salted through with fear."

Finally clipping on the double chute and sitting down, staring at the patterns of fields between his feet, Lindbergh committed himself by swinging down to hang beneath the bright yellow wing. Below was "nothing but space . . . terrible . . . beautiful."

In a moment he pulled the release knot and fell away from the Standard, until at last the parachute canopy filled out and he swung gently, noticing the redness of the sunset, the position of the landing field below, all fear gone. A second pull on the knife-rope cut him free again, to plunge on earthward, waiting for the tightening of the harness when the second canopy blossomed. There was a too-long wait and the ground rushed up, far too fast. Then, a jerk, and the final glorious ride to earth.

Harden was white when he ran up to see if Lindbergh was all right. The second chute had streamed and nearly did not open at all!

After that, Lindbergh was inwardly amused to find his stature had grown considerably higher than the six feet three inches he stood in his socks, and when visitors came to the field, they pointed to him and said to each other, "That's the parachute jumper!"

It had not yet been six months since young Slim, as he was known, got close enough to his first airplane to touch it, inside the plane factory at Lincoln. He had already decided to quit the University of Wisconsin and become an aviator, instead of going into politics like his father, a congressman from the Sixth Minnesota District, or becoming a farmer.

It was at the factory that he fell in love with the acrid smell of nitrate dope, the bright yellow wings stacked along the side wall, the big Hispano-Suiza engines on their test blocks, the slim, trim fuselages of the Standard JR1's that could do 86 mph in level flight and climb to 10,000 feet in only 20 minutes.

On the bright spring morning of April 9, 1922, young Lindbergh and a buddy from the sandy prairie country of Nebraska, Bud Gurney, eagerly climbed into the front cockpit of a brand new Standard and belted themselves down, side by side, for their first airplane ride. Their pilot was a man named Otto Timm, a Minnesotan who looked not unlike Lindbergh and who had been flying homebuilt airplanes since 1910.

The two boys held their breaths as Timm, all business, waved to the mechanic in front and yelled, "Contact!" A former barnstormer himself, Timm was now "chief engineer" at the Lincoln Standard plant, and his voice rang with authority.

Slim and Bud watched the mechanic throw the weight of his body into a strong pull on the varnished propeller blade, at the same time stepping backward with the grace of a ballet dancer. As the engine coughed and settled down to a rhythmic idling, the mechanic pulled the chocks from in front of the wheels and Timm gunned the ship forward, careful not to blow dust into the hangar where two other mechanics were painting wing fabric with the heady dope.

Gurney and Lindbergh nudged each other and grinned. This was the life! They looked back into Timm's face, half covered with big oval goggles and a tight cloth helmet. Timm ignored them, busily studying the wind, the

Lincoln Standard biplane, a barnstormers' favorite, was the ship in which Charles A. Lindbergh learned to fly.

clouds, the drift of shadows, the thousand and one things that are a secret part of the airman's world, the things he instinctively senses with a skill that is called airmanship. Lindbergh studied his face and saw all this, and was determined to be such a man.

The flight was over too soon. They had climbed high and swooped low over distant hills, chased wheeling hawks, and headed toward a drifting white cumulus cloud. The boys winced as Timm flew right through it, half expecting to feel an impact of fabric wings on the cottony substance. Toward the end of the ride, Timm banked the Standard over steeply so that the flying wires were parallel to the horizon, and when he pulled back on the oak joystick, they felt a tightening in their stomachs and a tugging that opened their jaws.

Ray Page, the company president, took Slim's personal check, and he was enrolled as the firm's one and only flight student. His instructor, Ira Biffle, a dark-featured, embittered veteran instructor left over from the war, did not share his student's poetic eye. Flying was simply a dirty, stinking, underpaid job, the more so since a close friend of his, Turk Gardner, had died in a crash.

Lindbergh had eight hours of dual instruction time in his logbook when he learned that the factory's only trainer was being sold to Erold Bahl. Furthermore, Page refused to let him solo without putting up a bond in case he cracked up on landing. He simply didn't have the money. He was at a dead end. It was then that Slim appealed to Bahl to take him along when he went barnstorming, and when Bahl reluctantly agreed, Lindbergh was launched as a barnstormer. Not as a pilot, at first; his jobs were to wipe down the ship at the end of the day, pull the prop through to start the engine, and coax the small-town crowds to fork over a few dollars for a few minutes in the sky.

One day Lindbergh volunteered to climb out onto the wingtip when they flew over town, to attract more curious customers.

"Go ahead," Bahl shrugged. "But don't put your foot through the wing fabric!"

Launched as a wing-walker and parachute jumper, Slim now rated equal billing with the pilot on the brightly colored handbills they tossed out of the cockpit while flying over Midwestern towns on a Saturday afternoon.

DAREDEVIL LINDBERGH! the handbills said. Slim then went on his second barnstorming tour, this time with a pilot named H. J. (Cupid) Lynch, a short, stocky man who flew a plane to Slim's liking. He decided early in the game that he could live longer by avoiding the crew of hard-drinking, swearing, grease-stained "airport bums" whose misadventures in the sky too often ended in the graveyard.

In the year 1923 alone, reported the authoritative *Aircraft Year Book,* gypsy fliers were responsible for 179 serious plane accidents in which 85 people died bloody deaths and another 162 were injured. Listed as "probable causes" were such chilling reasons as *stunting at low altitude; plane taken up with only a pint of gas; bad landing on bad field; plane plowed into crowd; stunt flyer failed to come out of barrel roll and tailspin* and *control stick broke.* By the following year, barnstormers were held accountable for two out of three fatal crashes.

Slim Lindbergh's second fling at barnstorming was an unforgettable experience, one that instilled in his heart a greater love for America than he had ever known. Winging low across western Kansas and eastern Colorado, he smelled the rich, warm pungency of the prairies in harvest, and he squinted at the vast expanses of bronzed land in a way that would line the corners of his blue eyes with tiny crow's feet.

The silver-hulled Standard seemed to belong in that part of the sky, winding its way jauntily between towering cloud pillars and dropping down to follow the muddy Platte and Powder Rivers, which smelled of damp algae and catfish, or skirting around the proud escarpment of the Big Horns, so full of color in the glory of October.

Lindbergh's eyes saw all this and loved it, for the grand panoramas of his country formed a giant relief map that supported the sky, and so flying over it, hedgehopping or higher up in the clouds, he was still a part of the land. The tug of gravity was ever-present, and when he tumbled down from the sky in free fall at the start of a parachute drop, it was like coming home. The flying season ended in Billings, Montana. Lindbergh packed up his parachute and shipped it back to Lincoln, then set out on a river adventure in a two-dollar boat on the Yellowstone.

During the winter months, Slim visited his father in Minneapolis, and there told him of his decision to buy an airplane and go barnstorming on his own the following spring. The elder Lindbergh saw the stubbornness in his son's eyes and smiled; he even signed Slim's note for $900, borrowed from a bank in Shakopee.

Lindbergh's first airplane was a beautiful, brand new JN-4D Jenny, painted olive drab and complete with two extra wooden propellers and a book of instructions, which he read over carefully after handing the salesman $500 at the Souther Field warehouse near Americus, Georgia. He memorized the specifications the way other youths memorized their girl friends' faces.

Heart of the Jenny, of course, was her V-8 engine, the Curtiss OX-5, an amazing powerplant developed by an engineer named Charles Kirkham at Glenn Curtiss' Hammondsport (New York) factory, where thousands had been mass-produced during the war. Developing 92-horsepower at 1300 rpms, the OX-5 weighed 434 pounds, while the gross weight of the whole ship was 1920 pounds, 50 pounds lighter than the Standard.

Flying the Jenny would be a new experience, Slim realized. The Standard's Hisso engine, rated at 150-horsepower, gave the JR1 a sea level speed of 86 mph, compared to about 70 for the Jenny. And as neither engine was supercharged, the higher you flew the slower you went.

Lindbergh hadn't been in the air since October and felt rusty, and what's more, he had never soloed, having only handled the controls of the Standard a few times when Bahl wanted to catnap. Hence, his first solo hop was nothing he would ever brag about, for on landing, he bounced back into the air and had all he could do not to groundloop.

Taxiing back to the hangar, he was embarrassed to find a stranger standing there, watching him. But the stranger didn't laugh; he was there to help him check out. After a few more circuits and bounces he was advised to wait until the air grew still at dusk. At last, going up alone as the sun sank over the Chattahoochee, Lindbergh began to feel at home in the Jenny. He flew in lazy circles over the Georgia countryside until the shades of night rendered the landscape flat and shapeless. Then he reluctantly idled the engine and glided down the sky to land. A watchman, alone on the field, came up grinning widely and congratulated him for "flyin' higher than any other fellers did!" Lindbergh accepted the compliment happily, then began to think of the future.

For the next year, Slim Lindbergh would follow the barnstormer's trail as he had planned, through the deep South and back up north to the Nebraska and Minnesota country he loved. Wisely, he waited until he had accumulated some five hours of flight experience in his Jenny at Souther Field before venturing off to join the gypsies of the airways. At that, in Meridian, Mississippi, he came close to killing himself and his first passenger.

His fare loved it, though. A huge man, he had eased himself into the front cockpit, and Slim had had to remove the control stick to make room. "Go ahead and do any nipups you like, son," he yelled. "I flew with the Lafayette Escadrilly!"

With close to three hundred pounds extra weight, Slim felt the Jenny wallowing like a bull walrus over the soft cow pasture he'd chosen to operate from. He picked up the tail and opened the throttle wide. With a great leap the Jenny got off the ground just in time to hurdle a split-rail fence. He mushed along, barely above a stall, unable to rise higher until crossing the crest of a ridge. Then he dove down into a small valley, gathered speed and managed to struggle back around and land.

"That's the stuff for me!" the big passenger boomed as he stepped out. "I shore like that there flyin' right off the ground! Scared hell outa the enemy that way, I did!"

Lindbergh swallowed and tried to smile, wiping sweat from his face. It was obvious his fare hadn't realized how close to disaster they'd been.

Early the next morning Lindbergh was off again for greener pastures. His goal was a little town 125 miles west of Meridian, but somehow he ended up 125 miles to the north, following a new compass he hadn't yet installed. Worse, a severe storm front was rolling toward him, and there was nothing to do but set down in the nearest field. It looked nice and green from the air, but he rued his choice, learning a lesson the hard way. Green grass means wet, soft earth, hidden stumps and ditches. He hit a ditch and nosed up on the propeller, which splintered to bits.

When a spare propeller arrived, Slim installed it, made a short test hop and then had time to earn a few dollars hopping passengers before moving on. On his last hop he took up a farm hand whose fare had been paid by two friends who thought it would be a fine joke if Daredevil Lindbergh scared the wits out of him. Slim agreed, although he'd never done acrobatic flying before. He tried a loop, but didn't have enough speed to get over the top. The Jenny fell off on one wing and wallowed back down the sky, much to his embarrassment and disgust.

Learning as he flew, Slim Lindbergh slowly added new maneuvers to his repertoire and practiced them daily at the end of a cross-country hop to a new town. It served both to sharpen his own flying and to bring out the customers.

Flying up into Arkansas, the Jenny pointed its nose west over Fort Wayne and headed into the Panhandle country of Oklahoma and Texas, then swung up into the Kansas wheat country. At Alma he survived his second crash landing, which occurred when his left wing hooked on a rock hidden by the tall grass in the field he had picked out for an airport.

Sleeping beneath the wing, Lindbergh rose early, patched the torn wingtip with fabric and dope he carried with him and moved on toward Lincoln, Nebraska, to say hello to his old friends there and show off his new plane. There Bud Gurney joined Slim and together they barnstormed west through Nebraska and into Minnesota, where for the third time his Jenny came to grief. Heading for Shakopee to see his father, he ran into a heavy rainstorm that soaked the OX-5 and drowned out three cylinders. His engine sputtering sadly, Slim headed down for the nearest field and plopped the Jenny into swampy terrain. This time the Jenny nosed over completely. He wired to Americus, Georgia, for his second spare propeller.

Finally reaching his home town, Lindbergh offered to fly his father around the state on a political campaign tour. It was a short, sad experience that ended within twenty-four hours when something went wrong mechanically with the temperamental Jenny and the Lindberghs crashed to earth at Glencoe. The local newspaper quoted C. A. Lindbergh, Jr., as telling their reporter that "the mechanism had been tampered with."

Slim's father escaped with a pair of broken glasses and a bloody nose, which came from striking the instrument panel, and went on to complete his campaign by automobile, but he was defeated at the polls, not that Slim didn't do his best to make up for what happened. Whenever an opponent stumped a town to make speeches, Slim was right there with the Jenny, hopping passengers and making so much noise that the politician couldn't be heard.

When October came, Lindbergh flew off to St. Louis to attend the Inter-

Charles A. Lindberg (right) discusses Curtiss pusher with another barnstormer, Al Williams, at Cleveland Air Races.

national Air Races at Lambert Field. There he ran into Bud Gurney again. Bud was making double parachute jumps himself now, the way Slim had done, but when he went up with Lindbergh, the Jenny couldn't lift the heavy load of the two youths and the two parachutes more than 1,700 feet. Bud jumped anyway and on landing broke his left shoulder.

To Slim Lindbergh, it was quite an experience rubbing elbows with the great pilots of the day. Lieutenant Alford J. Williams of the Navy, a crack acrobatic pilot, thrilled him by flashing over a speed course around three pylons at an average of 243.67 miles an hour. There was a minor aviation boom on, he discovered, and the price of Jennies had rocketed. He sold his ship to a man from Iowa, taught him to fly it, then in December picked up a bargain in an OX-5 Canuck, the Canadian version of the Jenny. The man who sold it to him had won it in a raffle, through a 75-cent ticket held by his young son.

After barnstorming around Illinois during the early winter months, Slim teamed with an auto salesman in St. Louis, Leon Klink, and together they headed south to seek warmer weather. Lindbergh had taken his entrance

71

examination for the Army Air Service at Chanute Field, near Rantoul, Illinois, and had until March, 1924, to finish barnstorming before being inducted at Brooks Field, Texas, as a flying cadet. Swinging down through Kentucky, Tennessee, Mississippi, Alabama, Florida, Louisiana and Texas, Slim cracked up only two more times—not bad for a gypsy flier.

One smashup was attributable to engine trouble, which led to a forced landing, and which in turn led to a shattered propeller. The other happened when Slim, who had made an emergency landing in a tiny pasture, tried to take off from the main street of Camp Wood, Texas, his forty-four foot wings barely squeezing between two rows of telephone poles forty-six feet apart. He missed. One wingtip hung up on a pole when he hit a bump in the road and around he went, the Canuck's nose ramming through the wall of a hardware store. When he offered to pay for the damage, the proprietor wouldn't hear of it. "Look at all the free advertising I got!" he declared.

Near Pumpville, Texas, Lindbergh and Klink ran into more misfortune when they landed near a railroad siding and in the morning had to hack a runway through hundreds of feet of sagebrush, cactus and mesquite. When they tried to take off, a Spanish dagger cactus impaled the plane's wing like a butterfly on a pin, ripping away the bottom fabric. Down they came again, blowing a tire.

Klink decided he had had all he wanted of flying and decided to hop a freight train for California. It was March, and Lindbergh was due at Brooks Field anyway. They shook hands and parted, and soon Slim was bouncing the battered Canuck down the sand strip, through the sagebrush, and into the air, one tire gone, the fabric on the lower wing shredded and a wing-spar cracked and held together with rope.

When he landed the Canuck later in the day at Brooks, mechanics and pilots gathered around it, shaking their heads in utter disbelief that it could even fly. Slim took their ribbing good-naturedly, but when the Commanding Officer showed up, it was another matter. Turning beet-red, the C.O. ranted, "Get that damned thing out of my sight!"

Lindbergh stammered an apology and got back in his Canuck, flying it over to a commercial airport. Four days later he was formally inducted as a cadet in the United States Army. On his first day he soloed—in a Jenny.

Shy, quiet, withdrawn, Charles Lindbergh was just another unknown gypsy flier until he astounded the whole world with his thrilling solo flight on May 20–21, 1927, from Roosevelt Field, Long Island, to Paris' Le Bourget Airport. At twenty-five, Slim Lindbergh, ex-barnstormer, became the most admired man in the history of aviation and an American phenomenon.

He had done equally dangerous things many times, as a wing-walker, parachute jumper and then as an airmail pilot. He had become "King of the Caterpillars" by saving his life four times in emergency jumps, more than any other member of the exclusive Caterpillar Club, and rated only scant attention. But his Atlantic flight threw a spotlight on him, and even the cynical press realized that a new hero was born.

For some sadistic reason, newspapermen delighted in making life hell for this introverted airman who saw visions too big for them to grasp and horizons too distant for them to comprehend. There was the time he was hired to fly film plates through murderous weather to give the Chicago *Tribune* a scoop over other papers on the story of the tragic rescue attempt of Floyd Collins, who was trapped in a Kentucky cave. At Chicago's Checkerboard Airport a figure appeared and identified himself as a *Tribune* man. In innocence, Lindbergh handed over the films—to the representative of a rival paper, the *American*.

Despite such treatment, America at large took Slim Lindbergh to its heart and worshipped him. Whereas he had been denied the right to take up a plane alone in Lincoln, when he wanted to make his first solo, the Navy Department ordered all stations to make available to him any plane he wanted to fly. And on December 10, 1927, Colonel Charles A. Lindbergh was decorated with the nation's highest award for valor—the Congressional Medal of Honor.

In truth, Lindbergh, the boy who barnstormed the wheat fields of Kansas and the hills of Wyoming, who crashed his way across the country on his first glorious trip with his own Jenny, became a part of the American dream. In an era of bootleg booze, gangsters, and moral decadence, he did what no other living person could have done. He gave his country something good, clean and honorable to admire and to love. And he started the biggest flying boom in history.

73

Martin and Peg Jensen pose with Earl Daugherty's Jenny in Long Beach. Despite good luck billikin insignia, Daugherty pulled off a wing and died in plane crash.

7/HAWAII OR BUST

MARTIN JENSEN, king of the gypsy fliers, began barnstorming out of San Diego in 1924 and became the first pilot to cover the United States, coast to coast. With Peg, his pretty, red-haired wife, Marty crammed more adventure into a decade than most airmen would encounter in a lifetime.

On an endurance flight over New York, while Peg flew the ship, Marty amazed press photographers in another ship by crawling out with a set of wrenches and working on the engine two thousand feet over the city. His aerial wanderings were first done in a clipped-wing Jenny, then in a Thomas-Morse Scout and in a few planes he built himself.

In 1927, Jensen was barnstorming the Hawaiian Islands when Lindbergh hopped the Atlantic, and so when the Hawaiian pineapple tycoon, James D. Dole, posted $35,000 in prize money for a race from the mainland to the Islands, Marty hurried back to San Diego to get a ship he felt could compete in the race.

The Dole Race became one of aviation's black marks, the most tragic event of its kind ever held. But it was a test of nerves and skill for America's leading barnstormers, and in the mad flying craze that began with Lindbergh's great flight, the race did have its hour of triumph. Here is the story of that ordeal as related to the author by one of only two pilots to reach Hawaii—Martin Jensen:

San Francisco lay a thousand miles behind us, and somewhere ahead lay a tiny pinpoint in the vast Pacific—Wheeler Field, Hawaii. The time was 10 P.M. Honolulu time, on that black night of August 16, 1927. Except for my navigator, Paul Schluter, I was alone over the Pacific graveyard, in bad trouble and frankly scared.

Our little fabric monoplane, the *Aloha*, pierced the inky night with only

75

my instincts as a barnstormer to guide her. Sure, I had a ball-bank gadget on my panel, but until now, I'd never learned to use it on a night flight through a suffocating fog blanket.

My throat felt as dry as sand as I peered left and right from the *Aloha's* cockpit—and saw nothing. And then I heard the whine of my Wright J-5 engine suddenly increase in pitch. Under my tense fingers, the control stick became rigid with the grip of rushing air. A feeling in the seat of my pants (the barnstormers' friend!) told me death was rushing up at better than two miles a minute. We were in a screaming spiral dive, that awful, sickening plunge that only gets worse when you try to pull out. I glanced quickly at my altimeter. We were still four thousand feet above the wind-lashed waves of the Pacific.

If we were in a spin, I thought wildly, I could recover. I had made a living as a county fair stunt flier and knew how to get out of a spin. An idea suddenly occurred to me; it seemed crazy, but it was the only way. I chopped the throttle, eased the stick back into my stomach until the *Aloha* shuddered, then slammed on full right rudder. The ship seemed to hang there in the black night, until with a sickening plunge the nose dropped and we were whipping wildly around and around, heading straight for hell.

I let her spin for maybe a thousand feet. Then I dumped the stick forward, got off the rudder and pulled out of the spin into level flight once more. My disorientation subsided and I exhaled slowly, wiped the sweat from my face and settled down to the toughest flying job of my life. I had to learn to fly on instruments, there in mid-Pacific, or die trying.

I felt a sudden jab in my back that made me almost jump out of the cockpit. I remembered Schluter, back in the cabin, strapped in among the extra gas tanks that cluttered up the space. In my excitement I'd forgotten about him. Paul was poking me with a broom handle, our only means of communication other than a clothesline.

I reached down and felt the line running over the pulley, and a note came forward to the cockpit, clipped on with a clothespin.

"For God's sake!" Schluter had scrawled hurriedly. "No more stunts until we get to the Islands!"

I had to laugh, despite the narrow squeeze we'd come through. I'd taken Paul on only three days before the great Dole Race from Oakland to Honolulu had begun. He had answered an ad I'd placed in the San Francisco papers.

At first I'd been skeptical because Paul, an "old man" of thirty-seven, was the oldest entrant in the race. And besides, he had never flown before. He had been a ship's navigator on a coastal vessel, the *City of Nome.* We were already on our way before I fully realized what that meant. Schluter's navigation tables were good only on the surface of the ocean—he had no way of correcting for altitude. In order to get a position fix, I'd have to drop down to within a hundred feet of those whitecaps while he shot the sun or the stars.

Our second navigation problem was simply that a great fog blanket covered most of the Pacific on that unforgettable night, and I was having trouble getting on top. Each time I would try to climb up through the overcast, the *Aloha* would dive off into a screaming spiral. I had no alternative but to grit my teeth and fight it out.

The engine coughed. I felt my mouth full of cotton again. That one tiny engine would have to keep running steadily for a full day—twenty-four hours —or else. But it caught hold again and I relaxed enough to go back to battling those crazy instruments. I was thinking about how, only a few months before, another J-5 engine had taken "Lucky Lindy" across the Atlantic, from New York to Paris, in 33½ hours. In fact, it was because of the great Lindbergh flight that I was now out over the Pacific, bucking rising headwinds, groping through the black night and flying by the seat of my pants.

James D. Dole got the idea for the great Pacific air race while returning to

Aloha, *ship built by Vance Breese, was flown in Dole Race by Martin Jensen and navigator Paul Schluter.*

Jensen finished tragic Dole Race after Art Goebel. They were the only two pilots to make it. Here Paul Schluter (left) and Jensen grin happily with Martin's wife, Peg.

Hawaii from the mainland on a Matson Line steamer, when the ship's wireless crackled with the news that Lindbergh had done it—flown the Atlantic solo. Dole well knew that Hawaii was a potential tourist mecca and he was not blind to the world-wide publicity another ocean flight, this one over the Pacific, could generate.

Already, of course, the route had been spanned by air; two years earlier, Commander John Rodgers almost made it in a flying boat, but navigated the last three hundred miles by water after a forced landing. In July, one month before the Dole Race was scheduled, Ernest L. Smith and Emory Bronte barely made it to the island of Molokai from Oakland before running out of gas.

From the start, Dole's "Pineapple Derby" was a disaster, plagued with unbelievably bad luck. The prize money—$25,000 for the winner and $10,000 for the next ship in—had worked like a magnet. Forty hopeful barnstormers dug down in their pockets and paid the entrance fee.

Unlike Lindbergh, these were not the thorough, precision airmen one would expect to find competing in so hazardous an event, a wild publicity stunt from the beginning. They came from the ranks of the barnstormers, men dazzled by the blinding picture of sudden wealth and fame, spurred on by the Lindbergh hero phenomenon. If Lindy had made it over the 3,600-mile route in 33½ hours, it should be a snap to fly 2,400 miles to hula-hula land nonstop. But there was a difference—Pacific headwinds.

By the time August rolled around the field of forty starters had narrowed to fifteen. Worried government officials, fearing a tragic end for pilots who had no over-water flying experience, insisted on rigid proficiency examinations. One pilot was flatly disqualified because his ship couldn't even carry enough gas to cover the distance. Two others had second thoughts as the countdown continued and wisely withdrew. Another three wrecked their ships on trial flights.

Ben Wyatt, a Navy lieutenant who was handling the pilot checks, made me promise to do exactly what Schluter would tell me to do. I agreed, reluctantly. I'd fly and Schluter would navigate, but first I wanted to find out if he was subject to airsickness. After all, it would be a rugged flight. I didn't want a greenfaced navigator on my hands.

I met Paul for the first time at the little tent city that had sprung up at the end of the 7,000-foot sandy runway on Oakland's Bay Farm Island, where the other Dole entrants worked feverishly getting their ships into zero-hour readiness for the race.

"Let's take a little ride," I said to Paul. We climbed into the *Aloha* and were quickly bumping down the takeoff strip. I thought then that we'd be lucky even to get out of there with a full load!

I climbed the *Aloha* out over San Francisco Bay, circled back near the Oakland Airport, and then suddenly shoved the stick forward. I heard Paul yell something, but held the ship in a dive until the airspeed climbed to a screaming pitch. Then I hauled back hard on the stick, until it seemed I'd sink through the seat. The little monoplane gracefully pulled up into a vertical climb, then arched across the sky and down again through a beautiful loop.

I spent the next ten minutes putting the *Aloha* through her paces and finally cut the throttle and glided back to earth. On the ground, Schluter managed a weak smile.

"You okay?" I asked.

"Fine!" Schluter said, then turned a light green. I could see he was going to be sick. He had spirit, though, and I knew I had a courageous navigator. Now, all he had to do was find Honolulu for me.

We were supposed to go on August 12, because on that night a full moon would rise at sunset, giving us some light to fly by all night long. We would need it. In 1927, instrument flying was still in its infancy. Smith and Bronte were experienced pilots and had good radio equipment, as did Army Lieutenants Lester J. Maitland and Albert F. Hegenberger, the only other aviators ever to make the Hawaiian Islands. The Dole Race pilots, on the other hand, were barnstormers by and large—men used to following iron beams and making sure there were plenty of cow pastures to land in if their engines quit.

Of the eight final starters, there was one exception—Art Goebel. A veteran Hollywood stunt pilot and a member of the famous Thirteen Black Cats aerobatic team, Goebel *was* an experienced instrument flier, and his ship, the Beech monoplane *Woolaroc,* did carry a two-way radio.

Goebel had been on a Universal Pictures studio location job when Lindbergh hopped the Atlantic. He decided immediately to have a go at the Pacific race when Dole posted his big prize money. Art had done all there was to do with an airplane, carrying wing-walkers like Gladys Ingle and Ivan Unger on thrilling plane changes and performing hair-raising newsreel stunts such as diving under the Pasadena Colorado Street Bridge with two girls standing on his top wing. But the Dole Race was an entirely different kind of stunt, calling for special new skills.

The moon rose full and bright on the night of August 12, but nobody was ready to start. We all signed an agreement to delay the race four days, and in that decision lay death.

At noon, the first ship took off. It was the *Oklahoma,* with Ben Griffin and Al Henly as crew. A crowd of ten thousand people cheered lustily as the *Oklahoma,* overloaded with gas, staggered off the end of the runway and headed for the Golden Gate.

The next two starters didn't even get off the ground. And from the way those ships, the *El Encanto* and the *Pabco Flier,* floundered in the sand, I could see trouble ahead for me. The fourth off was the *Golden Eagle,* a sleek Lockheed Vega piloted by Jack Frost and sponsored by the San Francisco *Examiner.* Frost lifted off gracefully and swung into the west as the next ship, *Miss Doran,* thundered off with three people aboard—her pilot, Augie Pedlar, her navigator, Lieutenant V. R. Knope, and pretty Mildred Doran, a Michigan schoolteacher.

Next went the *Dallas Spirit,* with Captain William Erwin, a World War I ace, and navigator Alvin Eichwaldt. Then it was time for Schluter and me to go.

Art Goebel, winner of the Dole Race in 1927, was a barnstormer too.

COURTESY ART GOEBEL

"All set?"I yelled back to Paul, crouched behind our fuselage fuel tanks.

"Honolulu here we come!" he yelled back, and I gave her the gun. Sand tugged at the disc wheels of our little monoplane. The propeller whirred furiously, but nothing happened. Half a dozen mechanics rushed out and threw their weight against the wing struts. Slowly the *Aloha* began to roll, coming to life as we bounced down the sandy runway and struggled into the air.

We flew along San Francisco's waterfront, gaining very little altitude as we passed through Golden Gate. Dead ahead I already could see trouble—a blinding white fog bank shrouded the Farallone Islands. I remembered what the government weather forecaster had told me—there would be a high-pressure ridge out over the mid-Pacific and the sky would be clear beyond that. The cloud deck, he assured me, wouldn't extend clear to the ocean.

Schluter had given me a compass heading to fly and instructions to stay within one hundred feet of the water so he could work his celestial navigation problems as we flew west. I remembered my promise to fly the way Paul wanted and stayed down low.

We didn't know until later what happened to the others, and it was just as well; I might have turned back then and there. Goebel, who left after us, of course made it to the islands and won first-prize money, but the others ran into serious trouble almost from the start. The *Oklahoma* had gone back to Oakland, her belly ripped open during her rough takeoff. The *Dallas Spirit* had given up and returned for similar reasons. *El Encanto* and the *Pabco Flier* had crashed on takeoff, and so only four planes were left.

The *Golden Eagle,* which made such a beautiful start, simply vanished at sea, and to this day her fate is unknown. *Miss Doran* returned to Oakland with engine trouble, but Pedlar decided to take a chance and start off again. The decision cost them their lives—the last ever seen of that ship was on its second takeoff, Mildred Doran blowing kisses from the window. So Goebel, the only instrument pilot, and I, though neither of us were aware of it, were the only ones left in the Dole Race, droning west into the approaching night of terror, one I will never forget.

I had faith in my ship, and even when the fog bank closed in around me, I believed we'd make it. I held close to my heading of 248 degrees, hour after hour. Schluter had suggested a great circle route, changing course one degree left every two hours, but he forgot to tell me to change course during the flight, and I didn't. I found out why later. Schluter had been unable to get

81

a sun-sight through the broken clouds, and when night closed in, even Polaris, the North Star, was hidden from view.

There was plenty for me to do to keep busy, and so I had little time to worry. My ears were tuned to the beat of our Wright engine, and from time to time I had to switch over the crossfeed to use up fuel evenly. The rest of the time I sat there hypnotized, staring at the earth-inductor compass. The *Aloha,* a $15,000 plane I'd bought from Vance Breese, flew well, and there was nothing to do but fly west toward Honolulu, where Peg, my wife, was waiting for me.

I remembered back to our barnstorming trips across the country and in the Islands, and how bravely she'd helped out by clambering over the wings to draw customers. I thought of our first venture, in San Diego, when a good crowd showed up to watch, but nobody had courage enough to fly with me. So I gave a ballyhoo pitch about flying safety, then told them I was going to go up to 1,500 feet, stop the engine and glide back deadstick to land right in front of them. I wasn't too sure I could do it, but I did. It worked like a charm.

If my engine quit now, I knew, there would be no place to land down below; nothing but miles and miles of open sea. It was warm in the open cockpit of the *Aloha,* directly behind the engine, but the orange glow from the exhaust stack was blinding; even when the moon rose four hours after sunset, I could see nothing but a dim, almost imaginary horizon. The fog bank had pressed us lower and lower until we were completely enveloped in it. I know now what must have happened to the *Golden Eagle* and *Miss Doran,* and even then I wondered how they were making out.

Blind flying without instrument knowledge or a radio beam to follow was deadly and foolish; we were at the mercy of the elements. Vertigo and mysterious sensory illusions began to confuse me as I groped my way through the blackness. Even my old reliable seat-of-the-pants technique couldn't be trusted; we could be flying upside down and not know it until too late.

My hands were sweaty as I nervously gripped the stick, straining to see ahead. Suddenly there was a jolt; we had struck the ocean! Shocked, I struggled with the controls as I felt the *Aloha* slam hard against a big whitecap, a blow that threw spray over the ship and almost wrenched the controls from my hands. Fighting against panic, I hauled back on the stick and rammed the throttle full open. I caught a quick glimpse of angry waves reaching for us as I pulled up into the choking fog once more. My one hope lay in climbing

82

on top of the cloud layer, which now stretched clear to the Pacific's surface, but any instrument pilot will tell you what it means to maintain control with only a needle, ball and airspeed to guide you, particularly if you aren't familiar with the trick of it.

We got past one thousand feet, then two thousand, and three thousand, and still no moon or stars. Then, passing four thousand feet, everything went crazy. I heard the scream of the wind, but couldn't figure out what the instruments were telling me. We were in a graveyard spiral dive! It was then that I took a chance and kicked the *Aloha* into a deliberate spin, simply because I knew how to get out of a spin.

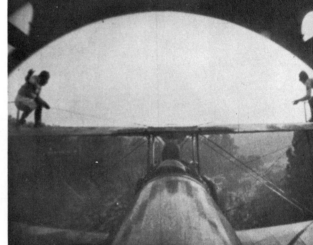

Art Goebel, flying for newsreel cameras, buzzes under Pasadena's Colorado Street Bridge with two wing-riders, Gladys Ingle and Shirley Calishak, on top wing.

COURTESY ART GOEBEL

We managed to recover, and three more times we went through the same agonizing experience, until somehow, by sheer desperation, I taught myself to fly by instruments. It was the world's quickest instrument flying course! I learned to disregard the nauseating vertigo that wanted to pull me off into those sickening spiral dives, and I discovered that I could keep the turn needle indicator centered by moving the stick gently to one side or the other.

Through the rest of the night I flew for my life—and Schluter's—with agonizing concentration on the needle, ball and airspeed, until at last a misty whiteness unfolded into a beautiful dawn. We were still alive and flying, but where were we? Schluter had not had a chance to check our position during the entire flight, but by dead reckoning I knew that we had flown long enough to be over the Islands by 8:30 A.M., Honolulu time. I looked at my watch. It was 9 o'clock!

I clipped a note to the clothesline and slid it back to Schluter. "Which way from here?" I pleaded. We were running low on gas, and I wondered if we'd picked up a tailwind and overshot our target.

Paul's note came back. "Circle until noon," it read.

I stared at it unbelieving. Fly in a circle for three more hours, when we were running out of gas? Then it dawned on me what he had in mind. It would be fatal to rush headlong in any direction, because we were completely lost; Hawaii could be on any of 360 different courses. We had to have a celestial fix, and the only way for Schluter, a ship's navigator with limited experience at that, was to get a sun shot at high noon.

It was deadly, flying in circles hour after hour, draining one auxiliary tank after another and perhaps throwing away any chance we had of making a landfall. But any plan was better than none, so we continued flying in circles until the main tank ran dry. The engine sputtered and almost quit before I could grab the wobble pump. A trickle of gas came from the outboard wing tanks.

Noon came. Paul, his face sweating, shot the sun as I circled once more, barely above the breaking whitecaps. Finally he clipped a note to the clothesline and sent it forward. I read it; Hawaii was two hundred miles away—to the south! That is, if Schluter was right!

I knew what had happened; by not changing course during the long night, and sticking to 248 degrees, we had gone too far north. Wondering if our fuel would hold out, I headed the *Aloha* south, leaned out as much as possible and waited. Every towering cumulus cloud became Diamond Head, and more than once I cried out, "Land ahead!"

84

At last I spotted a cloud that did not change shape—Oahu! Weaning every ounce of gas in a shallow letdown, I streaked in across Kahuku from the north, and over the Koolau range. I finally cut my power and glided noiselessly down the slope and, with a final roar, gunned across Wheeler Field, scattering the thousands of waiting people who were staring the other way, looking for ships that would never come in.

I pulled up and around in a fighter approach, then eased down and landed —28 hours 16 minutes after leaving Oakland. We had exactly four gallons of gas left—enough for one more hop around the field!

Schluter and I crawled out, exhausted but grinning. We embraced each other, intoxicated with the thrill of being alive. We felt certain we were the last in, having spent so much time circling north of Hawaii.

"The *Woolaroc* is over there," someone told me. "Goebel got in two hours ago. No one else is here."

Schluter and I looked at each other and understood. Goebel had flown on top of the weather the whole way and won first prize with a fine, professional job. For a barnstormer, it was something of a miracle that I had come in at all. The Dole Race was over, and Honolulu got its publicity—at a cost of ten lives.

First to die had been George Covell and Dick Waggener, two Navy officers who crashed to their deaths at Point Loma, near San Diego, while bringing their ship, a Tremoine Hummingbird up to Oakland for the Dole Race. Next was Arthur Rodgers, who failed in an attempt to bail out of his Bryant monoplane when it went out of control near Los Angeles, also en route to Oakland. The others were lost at sea—Augie Pedlar, Lieutenant Knope and Mildred Doran in *Miss Doran;* Jack Frost and Gordon Scott in the *Golden Eagle,* and Bill Erwin and Alvin Eichwaldt in the *Dallas Spirit.*

Peg and I returned to the mainland and took the *Aloha* on a cross-country tour—this time with plenty of landing fields underneath! The $10,000 second-prize money helped to pay for the ship, and ahead of us lay another ten years of living the life of gypsy fliers.

Since then I've designed helicopters and twin-engine executive ships and helped engineer giant Douglas transports, but the call of barnstorming is still strong. I'm working on a new design now, a little two-place job with swept wings and four engines, and who knows? Maybe I'll go barnstorming again with that!

Jensen won this $10,000 check for coming in second in Dole Race.

COURTESY MARTIN JENSEN

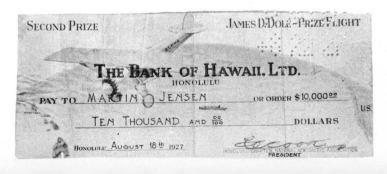

SECOND PRIZE   JAMES D. DOLE-PRIZE FLIGHT

THE BANK OF HAWAII. LTD.
HONOLULU

PAY TO MARTIN JENSEN   OR ORDER $10,000.00
                                                          US.

TEN THOUSAND AND 00/100 _____ DOLLARS

HONOLULU, AUGUST 18th 1927
                                          PRESIDENT

Barnstormer Dick Grace settled down in Hollywood where the pay was good. He specialized in crashing planes.

8/THE OLD AND THE BOLD

"THERE ARE OLD PILOTS and there are bold pilots, but there are no old, bold pilots," goes a barnstormer's adage. The same thing may be said of the "gypsy moths," roving bands of parachute jumpers who even more than men with wings surely knew that one misstep meant sudden death.

Now and then, in some remote airfield hangar, at some obscure county fair, you'll still find a few living old-bold ones, last of the breed of thrill-seekers, men who cheated death a dozen times, plus a few women daredevils also living on borrowed time.

Around rigging tables at scores of modern skydiving DZ's (drop zones), you'll still hear gossip about their amazing feats, and how they did the impossible and lived to tell about it. And about others who didn't. Much of the lore is legendary; most stories get better with retelling. But many were true.

There was dynamic Eddie Angel, brother of the famed barnstorming jungle pilot Jimmy Angel, a World War I Royal Flying Corps hero who joined the gypsy fliers in the 1920's and operated a cow-pasture squadron of death known as Jimmy Angel's Flying Circus. After a wild day's antics, the Flying Angels lured the suckers back to the field at night to witness Eddie's spectacular "Dive of Death"—a free fall plunge down the sky from five thousand feet while holding a pair of big flashlights.

"When I could see the ground," Eddie once explained to me, "it was time to pull the ripcord."

Then there was Bobby Rose, first of the great Hollywood stuntmen, who made women faint by falling backward off the top wing of a Jenny during a plane change. People shrieked in horror as Bobby tumbled down the sky head over heels toward certain death. Finally a 400-foot static line jerked open a hidden chute and Bobby floated earthward with cheers in his ears. "I used to plead with Sky-Hi Irvin to invent a ripcord and make my life easier," Bobby sighed recently. (Leslie Irvin did eventually become a successful parachute maker.)

Another old timer, Ed Unger, in 1967 celebrated his ninety-fifth birthday after a lifetime dedicated to barnstorming as a balloonist and parachutist. It was Ed who taught Sky-Hi Irvin to jump, and he still claims to have originated the idea for the manually controlled back pack parachute in use today.

Unger, Rose and many another old-time parachute jumper wintered in Venice, California, for two reasons—the weather was salubrious, and there it was that the early newsreel companies shot most of the early aviation thrillers. Few aerial stuntmen of the 1920's bothered with parachutes. They were cumbersome to lug around while clambering over the outside of Standards and Jennies while a camera ship flew in close, getting the action on film.

Duke Krantz, who originated the standing loop, scoffed at the idea of a "jump sack." After all, centrifugal force held him in place when he stood on the top wing all through a loop! Another barnstormer with disdain for the parachute was Walter Hunter of the Hunter Brothers Flying Circus. At a time when parachute jumps were standard fare at air meets, this team of four Oklahomans drew the biggest crowds by advertising their specialty—a "Thrilling Death Leap from an Airplane WITHOUT a Parachute!" The Hunters, a rugged band of grease-stained gypsy fliers, capped their show by dragging low across the field in front of the grandstand, Albert, Kenneth and John waving from the cockpits of their Standard biplane and Walter swinging by his knees from the axle. He'd let go and drop headfirst—right into a haystack.

Many a character used to drift into the old Venice Field hangar looking for stunt work during the Depression years. Of these oddballs, the strangest to Sam Greenwald, an International Newsreel cameraman, was a full-blooded Cherokee Indian, Chief Whitefeather, who showed up one day in the early 1920's, thick, black hair braided down his back, looking for wampum.

"Half a dozen pilots and cameramen were playing poker in a corner of the hangar when Whitefeather drifted in," Greenwald remembers. "He told us he wanted to hang by his pigtail from an airplane for $50."

To make sure that he could do it, they interrupted their game long enough to string the Indian up by his hair, which was tied to a rope thrown over a rafter. "We forgot all about him until that night," says Greenwald. "When we finally went back to cut him down, he was pretty mad, but in good shape."

The following day Frank Clarke, one of the top Hollywood stunt fliers, took Chief Whitefeather up two thousand feet over town. He swung happily in the wind while Sam shot movies of him from a camera ship. Clarke had visions of making a fortune by touring the country with Chief Whitefeather, the stunt to be sponsored by a hair-restorer company.

Whitefeather had other ideas. He wanted to try an even riskier stunt—a cutaway parachute drop with *ten* chutes. His idea was to open them one at a time, cutting away each one as it opened, then land with the tenth. Things went well as cameraman Joe Johnson ground away furiously, following him down the sky in another ship. But Whitefeather's sixth chute fouled; he plunged into a barley patch and was killed.

Walter Hunter (left) with brothers Albert, Kenneth and John, made up the Hunter Brothers Flying Circus. Walter dropped from their Standard biplane without a chute— into a haymow. Picture taken at Scott Field, Illinois, April 1924.

There was something quite dashing about carnival jumpers, handsome young fellows with pencil-line moustaches and a quick eye for pretty girls, heroes who lounged around small airports in white coveralls, white cloth helmets, and white sneakers. From habitually packing a thirty-pound parachute on their backs, they walked with a forward list, as if encountering a stiff headwind.

Such a barnstormer was Jimmie Goodwin, a veteran jumper and Hollywood bit player who added to his costume a pair of canvas batman's wings and a cloth stabilizer between his outspread legs to enable him to descend in spirals. Hank Coffin, a flier who used to take Jimmie up to jump altitude, claimed with a straight face that he once glided all the way down from ten thousand feet, over Big Bear Lake, to Alhambra Airport, seventy-five miles away! There are probably less than half a dozen batmen left today, and the work isn't steady, but before World War II no flying circus was complete without one.

Cliff Rose, another barnstorming jumper who knows what it's like to fly like a bird, made his first canvas wings at seventeen to become the world's youngest professional batman. When the regular performer didn't show up at a Long Beach air show, Rose bought some sailcloth and rigged an outfit that looked fine, but he wasn't too sure it would work.

Barnstormer Jimmie Goodwin built birdlike wings, became a batman.

At ten thousand feet over the airport Rose stepped out of an Aeronca, spread his arms and legs and felt a freedom he had never experienced before. He related the story to me this way: "I knew from the sound of the wind that I was diving faster than I ever had before in thirty standard jumps. I gripped the hand holds on two broomstick arms and pulled up, drawing the canvas taut. I spread my legs apart and there I was—a batman!

"I decided to try a spiral dive. Cautiously, I raised my right arm and dropped my left, then lifted my head, so that I was a sort of human corkscrew. Below me, the earth began to spin like a top. I was flying!

"I tried a loop next. Both arms extended rigidly, I lifted my head and arched my back. I tumbled over backwards with an easy mushing feeling. From the ground, they said I looked sensational!

"I was so busy trying out my wings I almost forgot about my parachute. In alarm, I realized I was so close to the airport I could see the yokels' faces. I yanked hard on the D-ring, too close for comfort. I hit the ground seconds later."

To prove he was really flying and not just falling erratically, Rose added an extra canvas pocket and filled it with red flour, then painted the blue sky with streaks of slashing red.

There is a bad joke about the fellow who bought a parachute and was told by the salesman that he could bring it back and get a refund if it didn't work, but it really happened to Rose.

"I'd organized a jump team billed as the Cliff Rose Death Angels, and I was making a long free fall. I waited almost too long to pull, trying hard to zero in on a forty-foot ground target. As luck had it, the chute streamed and failed to blossom. I barely had sky left to hit the emergency chute, and while I missed the spot, I lived to take the big twenty-eight footer back to the complaint desk. They cheerfully refunded my money."

Among other famous batmen were Clem Sohn, the first man to use canvas sails for body gliding (and first to be killed doing it); Leo Valentin, France's famed "human bird," who also died a victim of his crazy contraption, and Roy "Red" Grant, who made headlines by sailing above Niagara Falls from the United States to the Canadian side and back on homemade wings.

Not all barnstorming jumpers were killed by falling. There were other danger zones around small-town airports that took their toll of lives. Gladys Roy, a pretty wing-walker and jumper with nerves of steel, thrilled many an audience with her leaps into the wild blue yonder, which ended with her landing daintily and reaching for her compact. In Youngstown, Ohio, on August 15, 1927, Gladys lost her life—by accidentally walking into a spinning propeller.

Perhaps the world's greatest raconteur and authority on *Americana barnstormiana* is the irrepressible Louis "Speedy" Babbs, a still-active old-boldster who as much as anybody enjoys hangar flying tales "spun from whole cloth for the benefit of younger pilots, especially those who recently soloed."

Speedy will tell you about the twin brothers who in the '20's almost set a cross-country record of twenty hours in a Jenny, East coast to West. One brother, in a blaze of publicity took off from New York in a Jenny, after a

Cliff Rose, without a parachute, jumps from an airplane.

$5,000 prize. On the side of the ship was emblazoned its name: *Soul of Africa*. He waved farewell to the newsreel camera ship and winged off into the night—landing in a Pennsylvania cow pasture after dark. At dawn, the other brother arrived in Seattle, having taken off in another Jenny from a small town fifty miles to the east. Things went well until the award banquet, when newsreels of the departure and arrival were shown the admiring audience. The last scene showed Jenny No. 2 setting down at Seattle's municipal airport, the pilot climbing out smiling broadly. Behind him, in large letters on the fuselage, he had painted, *Sole of Africa*.

Speedy remembers an Army pilot named Weaver, stationed in the Canal Zone, who had several forced landings over the ocean. Each time he hit, his ship had nosed over. Finally he figured a way to lick the problem—the next time his engine quit he would glide down inverted. When his ship nosed over, there he would be, right side up!

Wild as some of the hangar flying tales were, Speedy heard few that could top his own personal experiences at cow-pasture dedications in the late 1920's and early 1930's. In his career as a stuntman Babbs broke only fifty-six bones, a few at a time, and so considers himself pretty indestructible. He started out to be a mere pilot, learning to fly in 1925 with Waldo Waterman, a pioneer birdman, but he couldn't raise enough money to buy an airplane. He invested in a $35 parachute instead.

"I helped dedicate more cow pastures than you can shake a control stick at," says Speedy, "not only doing parachute jumps and wing-walking, but some fancy rope ladder stunts, hanging from a Canuck by my feet and picking up a flag from the ground, and so forth."

His first "break" came at the dedication of San Bernardino's Tri-City Airport in Southern California on October 13, 1928. "I was supposed to ride the top wing of Bob Crooks' Curtiss Oriole, and while upside down in a loop, trickle off, fall free and open my chute as close to the ground as possible. It had never been done before."

Perched on the top wing, Speedy's skinny body nevertheless created such drag that Crooks barely got off the ground, flying *beneath* power lines you'll find at the edge of any small airport. "I had to duck to miss 'em!" he says.

Climbing finally to 1,700 feet, as high as the ship would go, Crooks dove for speed and mushed up through a loop. At the top Speedy slid off, and when he got low enough to hear the spectators screaming he reached for the rip cord. It wasn't there. It had fouled underneath his chest pack.

"With the same motion I jerked the rip line on my spare chute. It opened with a jerk, broke three shroud lines and split from the center to the lip, and then I hit the ground. I hit so hard I believe my tracks are still in the center of that airport!"

Speedy went to the hospital with two crushed vertebrae that left him paralyzed for weeks, but when he got out he went right back to the same airport—and opened a school for jumpers.

"I also did some more wing-walking, and once my dad was watching me. This lady next to him says, 'That man must be crazy up there! When he gets down I'd like to see what he looks like!' Dad says, 'Lady, stick right with me and I'll introduce you. He's my son!' "

With his back not fully healed, Speedy decided to forego parachuting for a while and take up something tamer. So he bought a motorcycle and had a big steel mesh ball erected at Ocean Park Amusement Pier, next to Venice, where he set a world record by looping the loop on the motorcycle inside the "Globe of Death" five hundred times in a row.

It was 1932 when Speedy made further headlines with a wild Fourth of July pyrotechnic parachute stunt that literally backfired and darned near killed him. And grabbing headlines wasn't easy that week, for big things were happening everywhere: Franklin Delano Roosevelt had just won the Democratic Party's nomination for President in Chicago, Amelia Earhart had made a forced landing near Los Angeles, Jimmy Mattern and Bennie Griffin were off on their round-the-world flight, Jean Harlow and Paul Bern were honeymooning in Hollywood and Norma Talmadge was suing Joseph Schenck for divorce.

All this was brushed aside on July 5 when the Santa Monica *Outlook* bannered the story: HUMAN SKYROCKET SERIOUSLY BURNED!

Speedy had made a deal with the Venice Pier manager to jump from an airplane at night and set off a bunch of fireworks on his way down. He went from airport to airport, looking for a pilot to take him up, but was turned down cold.

94

"I found out later that the CAA had threatened to ground any pilot who took me up," he recalls. "Finally I found a guy who would do it—he needed the money to lift a mortgage on his plane."

Speedy's angel of mercy was Chuck Sisto, a barnstormer who later made headlines himself as an airline pilot by accidentally, when his trim tabs stuck, doing half an outside loop over Texas with a DC-4 loaded with terrified passengers.

Sisto flew Speedy up to eight thousand feet over Venice Pier in the early evening and found the pier obscured from view by a three-thousand-foot cloud layer. Babbs decided to jump anyway, needing the money, so he crawled out to the wingtip, waved good-bye to Sisto and did a pull-off.

Hanging from his feet was a hundred-pound gunny sack full of star bombs and powerful red-white-and-blue flares, and a big inner tube for a life preserver. "I thought I'd light a couple of star bombs and see how the fuse was timed for distance," he relates. "The first bomb I lit dropped sparks inside the sack and all hell cut loose. The inner tube caught fire and blew out, and I set it swinging so that it would only burn me as it passed below my feet. The star bombs were blowing up inside the sack and my clothes caught fire. The only way to unload that sack was to reach inside and throw the stuff out—I'd left my jackknife at the airport.

Airport dedications drew barnstormers like flies. This is Union Air Terminal near Hollywood.

"Many of the pieces exploded in my hands, and I could smell my own flesh burning. But I hàd to keep on going—in the bottom of the sack was a large detonating bomb that was to be the finale. I knew that if that bomb exploded while still in the bag it would also blow me into little bitty pieces. How I did it, I'll never know, but I finally got it overboard . . . and you know something? It never did go off!"

The irony of the occasion was that all this action took place high above the cloud layer. Says Speedy, "No one saw it but me. My only regret was that I was the only one who saw that magnificent display!"

Meanwhile, back on the ground, people got tired of waiting and started to go home, which prompted the worried pier manager to call the airport. When Sisto informed him that Speedy had jumped half an hour before, rescue boats hurried out and picked him up, more dead than alive, two miles offshore.

Speedy was amused to read his own obituary in the Los Angeles *Times,* whose report of his death was, as Mark Twain once put it in a similar circumstance, greatly exaggerated.

On December 17, 1933, on the thirtieth anniversary of the Wright Brothers' first flight at Kitty Hawk, Babbs dreamed up another spectacular that almost cost him his life—the "Sky-Hook-Pendulum-Cloud-Swing." Speedy threaded three parachutes onto eight hundred feet of rope, one atop the other, with the nebulous idea of doing a pull-off at eight thousand feet and swinging down the sky in giant half-mile arcs while burning smokepots, so the folks on the ground could follow him.

For added insurance, he fortunately carried an emergency pack. The thought of landing at the end of a half-mile downswing unnerved even this cool character.

Things started off well. He crawled out onto the wing and clipped the rope to his harness, then released the triple chute rig, which finally jerked him into space.

"After falling long enough for the slack to be taken up, nothing happened," he remembers. "I grabbed the rope to relieve the shock on my harness and pulled in a few feet of it. The rope felt strangely slack, so I made a few more overhand grabs and there I was, holding the frayed end! It had broken about twenty feet above me!"

With more than three thousand feet of the sky already used up, Speedy

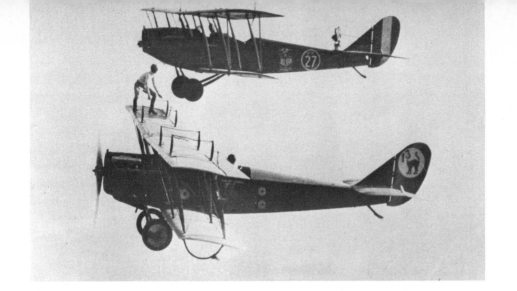

Wing-walker Gladys Ingle makes plane-to-plane change without a ladder. She climbs from top wing of Bon Mc- Dougall's Jenny to Art Goeb- el's lower wing.

COURTESY IVAN UNGER

Gladys Roy, wing-walker, was killed when she walked into spinning propeller.

lived up to his name by grabbing for the D-ring. But a horrible thought flashed across his mind: his life now depended on an old canopy that had been repeatedly immersed in sea water and hadn't been repacked in months.

"It opened like a charm, though," he says. "To keep my act from being a total flop, I lit the smokepots anyway, then spun the chute all the way to the ground—right in front of the grandstand, naturally."

Speedy's other chutes meanwhile drifted to earth miles away, and before he could locate them, one had been stolen. The next day he tried the stunt again with the two remaining chutes and got involved in still another adventure. Due to a stiff ocean breeze, he had decided to jump out over the Pacific Ocean, hoping to be blown back to the airport by the time he reached terra firma, but a lower wind-shift tricked him.

"Through force of habit I put the soles of my shoes together and took a drift sight between them. I was drifting out over the bay, instead of in toward land! I whipped out my sheath knife, cut loose from the two chutes and dropped, keeping my eye on the mountain ridge inland. When I had dropped to a level I was sure was dead air I popped the emergency chute. I took another drift sight; I was slowly drifting shoreward toward the airport, though still too far out over the bay for comfort. But my luck held and I landed within twenty steps of the water's edge."

Eventually Speedy recovered all three chutes, but he never again tried the "Sky-Hook-Pendulum-Cloud-Swing."

Another of Speedy's great ideas that didn't work was something he dreamed up and sold to Paramount News. ("When I was broke I could always sell Paramount News a stunt," he says.)

98

"First I sold Spud Manning on the idea. We were to go up and jump out of a blimp—and swap parachutes on the way down."

Due to a misunderstanding, the camera ship pilot thought the blimp was only up for a rehearsal (*nobody* would attempt such a fool stunt without practice!), and so the boys waited up there at four thousand feet in the big sausage while the camera crew went to lunch.

"Our heavy chutes and harnesses got mighty uncomfortable, so we took them off and played a game to kill time . . . see who could lean out the door the farthest. That wasn't too much fun, so we tried hanging by our hands, dangling our bodies in space, until the pilot, turning green, pleaded with us to put our chutes back on."

When the photo ship finally got off the ground, Spud and Speedy jumped together but missed, by a wide margin, coming close enough to trade chutes.

Speedy: "The next day I tied a mile-long linen string to my harness and rolled it into a ball, which I threw to Spud as we floated down. He was supposed to reel me in to where we could unbuckle and swap harnesses. But the string broke."

On the third try Lady Luck was either with them or against them, depending on how you want to look at it, for errant winds kept them from risking their lives in a foolhardy stunt that could have been the death of both of them.

Spud Manning, in fact, was one of Speedy Babbs' four partners to die in action, drowning in Lake Michigan when his plane ran out of gas during the 1933 World's Fair. The first of them to go had been Jimmy Young, who lost a struggle against a windstorm that blew his parachute out to sea. Next was a jumper named Curly Wells, another barnstorming gypsy moth. His last partner, Jimmy Pate, waited too long to pull the rip cord on a delayed drop and left his mark in Natchez, Mississippi.

Incidentally, Jimmy Pate's jump pilot was J. O. "Doc" Dockery, an old-time barnstormer the author fondly remembers from World War II days when Doc ran a cow pasture operation at a small field near Stuttgart, Arkansas, an advanced Glider Corps training base. Due to the usual sort of wartime foulup, the AAF had provided 1,600 student glider pilot trainees with only *four* CG-4A boxcar gliders. To keep their hand in, the students used to rent Piper Cubs from Doc Dockery and buzz freight trains chugging along the

After fracturing his spine, Speedy Babbs temporarily gave up exhibition jumping for something safer—motorcycle riding.

Missouri & Arkansas Railroad tracks. A favorite game, to the discomfort of the engineer, was to try to land on a moving flat car on a straight stretch of track.

One of Speedy's pals who worked for the Paramount News thrillers was a carnival escape artist named Joe Campi, who came up with the remarkable idea of having himself nailed inside a box slung under the belly of a Hisso Jenny. He was supposed to be dropped from eight thousand feet, then pull a release rope that would let the box come apart so he could parachute down.

"Well," says Speedy, "Joe dropped fine, but due to air resistance, the release jammed. Joe literally kicked that box to pieces and got out just in time."

Another of Speedy's crowd was Bob Coy, whom he calls "the best precision jumper I ever saw drop out of the sky."

One time down in Pensacola, Florida, Speedy recalls, "the local television studio asked Bob if he could land on the lawn at the studio and then walk right in for an interview. He said he could and we got him the necessary clearances, but the airport control tower neglected to tell the Navy what we were doing. It was at the time of the Bay of Pigs incident and Fidel Castro was threatening to bomb Florida cities. There were lots of clouds that day, but I found a hole and dropped Bob through it. He opened up and slipped his chute to land about fifty feet from the door of the TV studio, right on the sidewalk.

"As he'd planned, Coy rolled up his chute, tucked it under his arm and ran inside, right into the camera lens, for a video tape that was to be broadcast later that day. By coincidence, somebody with a vivid imagination driving past saw Coy drop out of the sky and run into the studio. He stopped and grabbed a phone and called the Navy base, sure it was a Castro invasion, reasoning that invaders would naturally take over communications first. Well, they scrambled every plane they could, but by that time I'd landed. We both caught hell."

The last time Babbs and Coy worked together, Coy jumped in a high wind at Key West, Florida, and broke his leg when he slammed into his own parked truck. The next day Speedy went to the hospital to cheer him up, but he couldn't get in; it was after visiting hours, a nurse told him. So he turned his collar around and tried again with another nurse.

"She almost broke her arm helping me when I told her I was the Reverend Babbs. Bob and I bowed our heads in silent prayer, and I slipped this fifth of one-hundred octane Southern Comfort between his sheets. That night Bob got high and fell out of bed chasing a nurse, his leg cast still tied to the ceiling. They found him that way the next morning, sleeping happily."

Some parachutists, it occurred to Speedy, are born to lose. Others adopt a philosophy of life and death that makes it possible to really enjoy things like the sport of skydiving, which, incidentally, Spud Manning invented when he was a barnstorming gypsy moth. Speedy worked out his own philosophy, after a near-fatal spill on his first motorbike prompted his father to give him a stern lecture about risking his neck foolishly.

"I told him we all have to die sometime, and anyone who is afraid to die, dies a thousand-and-one-deaths, while those who don't worry about it only die once, so we might as well have a bit of fun before the coming event!"

His friend, Bob Coy, it turned out, was not a born loser. In the summer of 1967 he was one of only two survivors rescued from the storm-lashed waters of Lake Erie following a tragic mass-parachute jump that took fourteen lives. An overcast sky had hidden their watery grave from the jumpers until it was too late in their free fall to alter their fate.

101

Frank Hawks barnstormed Mexico, flying payrolls over bandit country.

9/SOUTH OF THE BORDER

THE LEGEND HAS GROWN that barnstorming was strictly an American institution, as homespun as apple pie, maple syrup, hamburgers. This has led, in fact, to a derisive image of gypsy fliers as a wild bunch who turned handsprings for hamburgers and somersaults for sandwiches.

To go back to 1919 for a moment, listen to the pitch of a copywriter for the Aircraft Engineering Corporation who saw the skies full of American eaglets: "The most encouraging sign of the future of aviation is the large number of former army and navy fliers who are coming back into flying for sport, and as a profession.

"The war was responsible for the rapid training of many thousand men— the best blood of the nation!—who are generally recognized as the most skillful, resourceful and daring pilots in the world.

"When these men left the service, their interest in flying did not cease. On the contrary, they are more eager to fly than ever before. The call of the air is irresistible. They will fly, henceforward, just as in past years they played polo and owned speed boats and rode to the hounds. . . ."

You believe it?

The way Benny Howard remembers barnstorming was not exactly as a picture of members of the polo and yacht club set too bored with life to bother with anything less than a flying yacht, or following the hounds in a Christmas Bullet.

"We used to put mothballs in our gasoline, supposedly to make the engine run better," Benny recalls. And not the least of the dangers of flying during Prohibition was getting shot at by hillbillies who took you for a "revenooer."

The first flush of excitement over taking a ride in an airplane wore off quickly, and after the first year of scouring the back country for rubes willing to take a chance on a hop over the old barn for a five or ten-dollar bill, those gypsy fliers who did not starve to death or kill themselves soon began eying the illicit liquor traffic as a more lucrative and exciting way of life.

One of this breed was a lean, hawkish Texas barnstormer named Slats Rodgers, who started life in Dark Hollow, Mississippi, and knew little or nothing of polo, yachting or other "blue-blooded" activities of the social set to whom advertising copywriters mistakenly tried to sell an aviation boom.

Slats produced a book once, with a Texas newsman who helped him spell four-letter (and bigger) words, a colorful writer by the name of Hart Stillwell. To Stillwell's credit, the story of Slats Rodgers, called *Old Soggy* after a home-built plane Slats flew as a boy, is one of the more memorable accounts of early barnstorming. It has become a part of American folklore. The way Slats told the story to Hart Stillwell, satisfying the customers who wanted to get their kicks in his Jenny became increasingly difficult:

"They got to wanting loops and other stunts, and finally lots of them wouldn't go up if you *didn't* stunt with them. It suited the hell out of me. I might have stayed with flying, I mean hauling passengers, if it had stayed the way it was. I was making money fast. But here came the gypsy barn-stormers from other parts of the country, horning in. It was easy to see that kind of money wasn't going to be around for many years. People would pay to go up once, twice—then they wouldn't pay any more. Before long you ran out of customers. So I kept in mind that I was hauling passengers mainly to build up the right kind of reputation for my ship. I wanted her to be a lady, above suspicion."

Slats, of course, had his eye on the Mexican border; there was cheap booze on the south side and booming oil towns on the north. Slats found he could pick up a case of Scotch for $20 in Mexico and get $50 a bottle for it from thirsty oil-field roughnecks any Saturday night.

Like Benny Howard, Slats soon found his Jenny the target of sniper fire, but this time the anti-aircraft batteries weren't manned by moonshiners, but by Texas border patrol officers who were quick to realize that Slats no longer was just an innocent passenger-hopper. He switched to night-flying, landing on remote dry lake beds lighted by flares made from wine bottles filled with kerosene.

Coming back, Slats improvised a unique cargo-drop that enabled him to make round-trip flights out of Mexico without running the risk of apprehension in Texas. What he did was roll the bottles (or sometimes watches—reputedly Swiss) in a sheepskin bedroll tied to the lower wing. He simply buzzed the drop zone and cut his cargo loose, right into the arms of the waiting customers.

One time Slats got greedy and paid the price; there was a big Saturday night celebration at an East Texas boom town and he was commissioned to bring in fifty gallons, a consignment worth a small fortune. Slats took a chance and lost; the Federals were waiting for him when he landed. They quickly tossed him in jail, locking up the liquor in a storeroom for evidence when he came to trial for rum running by air.

Waiting for his trial in the Dallas pokey, Slats once more convinced officials that he was simply a misunderstood aviator who had become the victim of circumstances, mostly economic. The jailer felt sorry for Slats and made him a trusty. Then—if you can believe Rodgers—he swiped the key to the storage room and made off with the evidence against him, selling it through the window bars to passersby at a profit.

Slats went on to become one of a group of barnstormers who settled down at Love Field, near Dallas, for the cold winter months and toured north when the geese began honking overhead. For a while he stunted in a fancy

"Mein erster Bruch!" (*My first crack-up!*) *World War I German pilot Max Holtzem walked away from this crash landing.*

Travelair, preferring the life of a gypsy flier to the perils of bootleg flying. A favorite stunt of Slats was to bounce his wheels on the runway in front of the grandstand and then pull up through a loop. Several times he misjudged his distance, but each time he cracked up a ship, his fame—and price—grew proportionately.

Looking back at those good years, Rodgers remembered: "I guess we were a strange lot, those of us who flew those old traps every Sunday at the field. Maybe we were sort of a mixture of the cowhand of the Old West, the hot rod driver of today, and the real gypsy. We thought we were as free as the birds when we got into the air, just as the old-time cowboy thought he was as free as the coyote. We deliberately missed death by inches, and we played the sucker wherever we could find him, which meant roaming the face of the earth like a gypsy."

If Slats Rodgers fancied himself some kind of a heroic figure, he wasn't alone. A good many of the barnstormers affected a studied individualism that represented a kind of mass protest against growing regimentation, if you care to look at them in the same way that the leather-jacketed motorcyclists or beaded hippies of a later generation are viewed. True, the world then was not nearly so complex, but there was sufficient reason for rebellion, and rebel they did, many of them heading south of the border into the life of romance

Princess Elly Jonescu and Hans Geberth ride wings of Max's Salm biplane in this thriller.

and love and music and new adventure they believed awaited them in Mexico, in Central America and in South America.

Frank Hawks, who had been a wartime flight instructor at Love, Taliaferro and Brooks Fields, took his discharge after the armistice and cleared out of the country, flying oil-field payrolls over bandit country in a Hisso Standard on the Mexico City-Tampico run, along with Jimmy Angel, who had flown with the Royal Flying Corps.

Even before World War I, barnstormers had sought their fortunes in Mexico, when flying jobs were as scarce as hens' teeth in the United States. Some, like Mickey McGuire, flew for Pancho Villa during the Mexican Revolution, and others, like Didier Masson, flew for the *Nationalistas*. Earning up to $100 a day, they sometimes allowed themselves to be "shot down" by the other side so their buddies would have a ship to fly on retaliatory raids. It didn't make much difference which side they were on, for their homemade bombs, carried in their laps in flimsy wood-and-wire pushers, seldom did any damage.

Unlike the other barnstorming mercenary pilots, Hawks decided against joining in the prolonged Revolution, as he had many friends on both sides and didn't want any of them to get hurt on his account. So, until things quieted down, he temporarily gave up flying and worked as an oil field driller.

In 1921, under contract to the Mexican Government, Hawks put together a flying circus to help celebrate the national centennial. He hired Augie Pedlar, an expert mechanic and wing-walker, and played a leading role in making Mexico air-minded in its early post-revolutionary days.

Some years later another troupe of barnstormers, broke and hungry, found themselves stranded in Tampico. They didn't have Hawks' understanding of the Latin temperament and so decided to sell their four Lincoln Standard biplanes to a Tampico banker who saw an opportunity of using them for shuttle flights into the booming oil fields at Tuxpan, ninety-three miles across the green jungles. Thus was born on August 20, 1942, the oldest Latin-American airline, Compañía Mexicana de Aviación.

Hawks finally took a job with Mexicana and flew down to Tampico from

107

Mexico City so many times he got to know every cactus on the route, but the day came when he covered the entire two hundred miles without one glimpse of the ground, on top of a solid overcast. On a routine trip, Hawks knew, there were rugged mountain peaks up to nineteen thousand feet high to climb over before starting to let down over the rain jungle of the coastal plain, but on this trip he had no way of knowing when it was safe to come down.

"I've faced death many times during the twenty years I've been flying," he recalled afterward, "but in thinking over all of those close calls, none of them could hold a candle to this one."

What haunted Hawks was that he felt sure he had picked up a tail wind, but he didn't dare drop down into the clouds until he was certain he was over the worst part of the mountains at Pachuca, normally a one-hour flight from Mexico City in his 75-mph Standard. For good luck he flew another fifteen minutes, then another five for insurance. He sucked in his breath, throttled back, and settled down into the blinding whiteness of the cloud layer, half-expecting a mountain peak to loom ahead of him at any moment.

Minutes passed and still Hawks was in the soup, getting lower and lower. Finally he saw something beneath the lower wing—water! He groaned. There was no telling how strong the tail wind had been. He could be as much as a hundred miles out over the Gulf of Mexico! Hawks quickly circled around and flew back over the course he'd followed, hugging the waves.

For what seemed like hours he nursed the Hisso along, saving fuel, until his engine began to sputter and threatened to quit. Straining his eyes to see ahead, he finally made out the distant shoreline. He landed at his home base with less than a gallon of gas left.

Jimmy Angel led an even more adventurous life during his Mexico barnstorming days. Like Hawks, he took a job flying payrolls over bandit country. He once told the author of this book the story of how a passenger in the front seat of his Jenny suddenly turned around and pulled a gun on him, five thousand feet over the Barranca de Cobre country.

"I'd brought him along as a guard, but I guess he got some ideas of his own," Jimmy recalled. "I was supposed to land somewhere down there, and I knew that the minute I did I was dead. He obviously meant to shoot me once we were on the ground, and take off with the gold. Well, it was his life or mine, so I rolled inverted and stuck my foot against the stick and shoved. The nose swung up hard. He popped out of the cockpit, bounced off the wing, and the last I saw he was grabbing air on his way to eternity."

One time Jimmy faced a ticklish situation that called for some fast thinking: a revolutionary leader tried to hire him to bomb the palace in San José, Costa Rica. Jimmy's pretty young bride, Marie, was staying in the hotel next to the palace, waiting to catch a plane back to the United States the next day. If he turned down the job, some other pilot would get it and could easily blow up the hotel by mistake, so Jimmy agreed to fly the mission.

Stalling as long as he could, he tinkered with the engine, cleaning the plugs and fooling with the carburetor, until the revolutionary began getting suspicious. Finally Jimmy told him he'd have to wait until dawn, which would be better because everybody would be asleep and that way they could more easily wipe out the opposition.

"*Bueno!*" snapped the leader, stalking off to attend to other matters. The next morning Jimmy was off the ground at first light, smiling to himself; during the night he'd got word to Marie to clear out in a friend's airplane. He buzzed over the palace, where President Teodoro Picado was sleeping, unaware how close he'd come to death. Jimmy zoomed off into the wild blue and headed south to continue his adventurous barnstorming career in Panama and Venezuela, where he operated the Jimmy Angel Interamerican Aviation Service.

On Holtzem's barnstorming tours, any backyard was an engine repair ship.

His subsequent search for a lost gold mine atop Auyán-tepuí, an awesome mesa in Venezuela's Gran Sabana country, is the tragic story of a man who followed a dream unto death, the elusive prize always just beyond reach. Briefly, it is the story of an old prospector named Bob Williamson who showed Jimmy a hatful of huge gold nuggets and offered to share his secret if Jimmy would join him.

Jimmy landed his plane atop the distant mountain at Williamson's direction, and sure enough, there it was—a mother lode!

Before Jimmy could go back and set up a claim, the old prospector was killed in a Panama waterfront fight, and never again could he locate it, although he spent more than two decades trying. He did find a magnificent waterfall, however, the highest in the world (3,280 ft.), which today bears his name—Angel Falls. In 1956, he was off again with new backing, heading back to Venezuela with fresh hope of finding his lost mine. Instead Jimmy found death, in a simple accident in Panama, which occurred when he tried to land in a stiff crosswind.

In 1968, a renewed effort to discover the secret of Auyán-tepuí Mesa was made with the organization in Los Angeles of the Lost World Scientific Expedition, headed by two veteran parachuting barnstormers, Dave Burt and James C. Hall, and an associate, George Waltz. This time the search was conducted by helicopters and with the more scientific goal of discovering new flora and fauna in this region made famous by Sir Arthur Conan Doyle's book, *The Lost World*.

His middle name was Orville and the Arapahoes called him Tall Feather, so it was natural that Edward O. DeLarm, a lad from the Big Wind River Reservation in Wyoming, should become the first full-blooded Indian birdman and end up in a real wild west adventure, as the first barnstormer to invade remote Patagonia in South America.

In Redwood City, California, DeLarm qualified for his pilot's license by flying with Sy Christofferson, a wartime builder of Jenny trainers. He then worked his way up as a respected test pilot for several aircraft manufacturers. After the Wall Street crash in 1929, DeLarm found opportunity wasn't knocking loud enough to do a drifting pilot much good, so he set out on the day before Christmas of that year on one of the longest overwater flights in history to seek his fortune below the equator.

Piloting a Sikorsky amphibian on a delivery flight from Roosevelt Field, New York, DeLarm winged southward to Cuba. There he gassed up and continued on to the Greater Antilles via Haiti, Santo Domingo, Puerto Rico, the Virgin Islands, the British West Indies, Trinidad, and from there up the Amazon to Para, Brazil, and across Uruguay to Buenos Aires. The flight blazed a trail that would open regular passenger and mail service, but DeLarm's Indian blood was restless, and on September 20, 1930, he moved on to greater adventures, taking off from Buenos Aires with six passengers on a 1,100-mile charter flight across the continent to Concepción, Chile.

DeLarm was amazed to read in the logbook that his craft was the same Fokker F-7 in which Amelia Earhart had winged across the Atlantic in 1928 as a passenger with Wilmer Stultz and Louis Gordon—the *Friendship*. It was then owned by one of DeLarm's passengers, all of whom represented themselves as just a bunch of homesick Chileans. What the pilot did not know was that they were armed revolutionaries plotting a takeover of the Chilean government, and that their baggage, 1,100 pounds of it, was mostly firearms and ammunition.

No sooner had they landed at Concepción than a small army surrounded the amphibian. This, it seemed to DeLarm, was not in the best tradition of welcoming committees, particularly for a flying machine named the *Friendship*. He was even more upset when they marched him off as a prisoner to await the outcome of a trial of his passengers for attempting to oust forcibly the incumbent government the hard way. They were found guilty, of course, and sentenced to fifteen years imprisonment in a leper colony on a Pacific island, there being no death penalty. Later they escaped to France.

DeLarm, considered an accomplice to the others in the dastardly plot, was held on a battleship during the trial and was later transferred to a military prison. He remained there for thirty-seven days, until one night when he noticed that the guards were celebrating heavily. When one fell into a drunken slumber, DeLarm lifted his keys, opened the doors and walked out to freedom. For the next thirteen days he made his way across the Andes, following uncharted trails and living off the land. He finally reached Zapala, Argentina,

111

and hopped a train back to Buenos Aires, reminding himself to check the passenger manifest more carefully on his next charter flight.

One of the most remarkable barnstormers in the entire Western Hemisphere was a self-exiled German national named Max Holtzem, who came to South America after the armistice for a simple but compelling reason—he loved flying, and under the terms of the Treaty of Versailles, flying was *verboten* in Germany.

He had done pretty well, as combat heroes go, as a pilot with the Bavarian Jagdstaffel 16, but even before that Max had been making aviation history as one of the real pioneers of flight in the Kaiser's conservative empire. A youth of twenty in 1912, Max built his own airplane, which resembled a Blériot monoplane but was underpowered, having a Delfosse rotary that could barely lift it off the grassy fields near his home in Cologne.

Against the wishes of his parents, Max enlisted with the Imperial Army

Holtzem (wearing goggles, top) instructed group of wild Turks in Austria, 1916, in an Albatros.
COURTESY MAX HOLTZEM

In 1916, Holtzem wrecked so many ships that Max's fellow pilots were wondering which side he was on. Here's what happened when a loop in a Pfalz didn't work out.
COURTESY MAX HOLTZEM

Air Service in 1913, and with the outbreak of war the following year was assigned to a Tauben squadron, flying over the front lines in Luxemburg and France. "Dueling in the air in those days was unknown," Max related to the author, "and the Huns and poilus saluted each other whenever they passed each other in the air."

To liven things up, Max decided to play a trick on his friendly enemies. "I attached an extension pipe to the end of my Very signal pistol, and as I passed the next French airman I showed him the profile of my 'gun' and fired it. The smoke and fire scared him immensely, to my great amusement." He was less amused the next day when the French pilot took a pot shot at him— with a real gun.

Because he showed great promise as a pilot, Max was commissioned as a test pilot at the Pfalz Pursuit Aircraft Factory at Speyer, where with Gnome rotary engines, the Germans were turning out carbon copies of French Morane-Saulnier monoplanes.

By 1916, with the factories humming along, the German Air Force needed pilots more than it did planes, so Max was transferred again, this time to the sole Bavarian air base, at Schleisheim, near Munich, as chief (and only) instructor.

"I alone was authorized to take up a brand-new model, the 14-cylinder, double-row Gnome Pfalz single-seater," says Max. "This aircraft, with its castor-oil burning rotary 'Schnurpser' engine, was a very special ship, to be used only for the defense of Munich."

When the Grand-Inspector of the Bavarian Air Corps arrived in his flashy car one day to inspect the hot little Pfalz fighter plane, Max spotted in the car a beautiful dashboard clock that he decided would look just great in the Pfalz panel, so while the visitors looked over the Pfalz, Max removed the clock. The Grand-Inspector raised hell when he discovered the theft, but after things cooled down, Max installed his prize in the cockpit, quite proud of himself.

He wasn't so proud the day he told his student pilots to watch from the ground while he demonstrated a low-level wingover in the single-seater Pfalz. He took off, climbed high over the snowy Bavarian countryside, then came buzzing along a road toward the flying field and pulled up sharply in a climbing turn. The engine misfired at the critical moment, and instead of diving

Max (right) didn't mind getting his hands dirty. Hans Geberth (left) and Princess Elly Jonescu, were wing-walkers. Henri Roger (next to Holtzem) was his "impresario."

back the way he had come, under control, the Pfalz shuddered, shook and spun in.

"I *walked* to the ambulance," Max recalls proudly.

As an acrobatic instructor, Max first had to teach himself how to loop and roll and do falling leafs before demonstrating the stunts to his students, many of them mustachioed Turks who flew airplanes the way they rode horses—full speed ahead. "I got cold feet the first time I tried a loop," he remembers. "I went into a bad tailslide—the Pfalz had no stabilizer or fin— and then I tried it again, successfully. I did twenty in a row."

Switching to the Albatros, Max adopted a personalized insignia on the side of his ship calculated to scare the enemy to death—a blazing comet with the name HOLTZEM slashed across the top. Back in combat for the long-awaited German offensive in March of 1918, Max was very discouraged to see his commanding officer, Lieutenant Heinrich Geigl, a hero with twenty-one kills, ram his Albatros head-on into a Sopwith Camel. "The British plane disintegrated, while the Albatros seemed unharmed. Then it began a steep turn, and one wing fluttered off before it plunged to earth at terrific speed."

114

Max didn't kill anybody in the shooting war, not even himself, but he did frighten the wits out of the good burghers of Cologne two days after the armistice by leading a flight of three Jasta 16 Fokker D-7's back from the front to his old home town.

"Down there I saw the beautiful spire of the Cathedral, the bridges, all the landmarks I knew and loved. They had come through the war unscathed, but now everybody thought Cologne was under attack!"

Max led the formation in trail over the rooftops and beneath the bridges that spanned the Rhine, then high-tailed out to the airport and landed, returning by taxi. It was a glorious flight, and the last he ever made in Germany. "The end of the war brought an abrupt end to all flying for German aviators," Max recalls. "But I had different plans. Because I loved flying and struggled so hard to become an aviator, I could not bear to give it up. My decision was to leave Germany if it meant that I could still fly. I went immediately to Argentina, in South America, and there flew at the military airdrome, El Palomar, near Buenos Aires."

Max was once again his old self, though he admits, "I was detested by some members of the French Mission who had come to the Argentine to sell their old war planes." There also he met Lawrence Leon, an American representing the Curtiss factory, "who was showing the Argentineans the beauty of his high-priced, but low-powered Jennies."

Max went to work building up a name for himself as a crack acrobatic pilot and formed South America's first flying circus, the Circo del Aire. It was the start of a whole new career for him, very much in the same way that returning Allied fliers had gone into barnstorming in the United States and Europe. And for a while he had the continent virtually to himself, or at least the sky above it.

Max did not get the idea for the Circo del Aire from the notorious Flying Circus of Baron Manfred von Richthofen. "The Baron prohibited aerobatics," he said. "He was a straight killer. He never once made a looping." Max did, though, often with a pair of fearless wing riders sitting on top of his Salm biplane, which was a copy of a German trainer built in Argentina and powered with a 100-horsepower Rhone rotary. One of his stunters was Eugen Geberth, a destitute wartime buddy who followed Max to South America

115

Princess Elly Jonescu was Max's girl wing-walker.

116

and joined the show. The other was Princess Elly Jonescu, a Romanian beauty and multilinguist who had found life boring in postwar Europe.

From 1921 until death parted them, Holtzem, Geberth and Princess Elly roamed from *ciudad* to *ciudad* and were billed by the Latin press as *Las Suicidas*. "People came from miles around to see us killed," says Max. Until Geberth finally obliged them by slipping and falling from a monoplane near Santiago, Chile, in November, 1924 (Max wasn't flying him that day), the Circo del Aire held a perfect record for aerial lunacy.

Most of their performances were staged at enclosed *sportivas* and race tracks, and one of Max's big crowd-pleasers was the old car-to-plane change that originated with the Fox-Movietone Newsreel stunt team, the Thirteen Black Cats, up in Hollywood. Because the cars had difficulty getting up speed to match Max's flying machine, he tied sandbags to the bottom of a ladder and swept low overhead, trusting to the stuntman to leap and catch it on the fly. Now and then one walloped the car driver on the head.

Max much preferred doing simple loops with Princess Elly and Geberth on the wingtips, because the ship was better balanced that way. These maneuvers were not done high in the sky, but virtually at ground level so that the spectators had to pay to get inside and watch Elly swooping past the grandstand below the roof tops.

Max did have trouble with Geberth, who insisted on using a long ladder on car-to-plane changes because the Gnome covered him with oil on a short one. On skidding turns, Geberth swung far out from beneath the landing gear until he could almost grab the wing skid. Once Geberth came close to having the ladder sawed in two by the propeller.

After Geberth's death, Princess Elly drifted off to seek new adventures, and in 1928 Max headed north to accept a job as a test pilot for his old friend Tony Fokker at Teterboro, New Jersey. Within two years the Depression had made it impossible for barnstormers to make a good living, and after a final show in Newport, Rhode Island, Max retired from active flying and moved to California to settle down. Now in his sunset years, he enjoys thumbing through several scrapbooks or threading a movie projector with a flickering old newsreel sequence of the Circo del Aire swooping low over an Argentine race track, back in the days when flying was so different. . . .

117

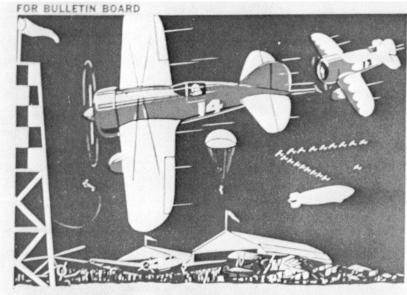

PACIFIC INTERNATIONAL
AIR PAGEANT

Auspices: NATIONAL AERONAUTIC ASSOCIATION

AIR RACES — WORLD'S SPEED DASHES
DAREDEVIL STUNT-FLYING

HEADED BY WORLD-FAMOUS AVIATORS

COL. ROSCOE TURNER   "IRON HAT" JOHNSON
America's Thrill Rival to Falesul and Udet

GLADYS O'DONNELL   U. S. and FOREIGN ACES

HOLLYWOOD TRIO
FRANK CLARKE — HOWARD BATT — PAUL MAENTZ

CURTISS-WRIGHT
FLYING FIELD San Mateo ● **SAT. SUN. DEC. 16·17**

CASH PRIZES for AIR RACES, STUNTING EXHIBITIONS,
SPORTSMAN PILOTS' EVENTS & WOMEN'S AIR DERBY

Obtain Entry Blanks at your Airport, or Wire or Write Committee Headquarters, Whitcomb Hotel, San Francisco
Visiting Plane-Pilots Guests of Committees at AVIATION BALL and AIR PAGEANT — Planes must arrive at Flying Field
before 11 noon daily — No Afternoon Landings Permitted.

ADVANCE PURCHASERS OF RESERVED SECTION AND BOX SEAT TICKETS FOR PACIFIC
INTERNATIONAL AIR PAGEANT WILL BE GIVEN INVITATIONS TO THE

AVIATION BALL CIVIC AUDITORIUM **Sat. Night, Dec. 16**
SAN FRANCISCO

BLANCHARD PRESS ● SAN FRANCISCO

Iron Hat Johnston was featured performer at Air Pageant with Colonel Roscoe Turner, Gladys O'Donnell and Hollywood Trio.

10/HERE COMES THE CIRCUS!

THE NEXT TIME you board an airliner, sit back in your comfortable, cushioned seat and settle down to watch a first-run movie or listen to music via the stereo sound system, pause a moment to reflect how it all began, back in the days of the barnstormers.

"Ladies and gentlemen," your airline captain will say over the closed-circuit speaker, "we are about to depart for a brief flight at an altitude of forty thousand feet. The weather is clear all the way, and we hope you enjoy your flight."

On May 25, 1924, hundreds of people traveled out to the airport in Lincoln, Nebraska, where Daredevil Lindbergh had learned to fly two years before. Gaudy posters had fluttered over town announcing a stupendous air show featuring races, stunt flying and parachute jumping. Besides the Lincoln Standard biplanes, five Army De Havillands from Fort Riley, Kansas, were there to introduce folks to the sky.

In that single afternoon, to help launch air travel, three Standards took 408 people into the air for the first time at three dollars a head. One pilot, Bob Cochrane of Casper, Wyoming, hopped 184 people. "At no time during the afternoon," reported *Aviation* magazine, "was there a lull in obtaining passengers. The new price of three dollars for five minutes seemed very popular, because in a number of instances the same passenger remained in the ship on landing and rode as often as four times in succession."

Much of this nationwide air-mindedness was traceable not to ex-military gypsy fliers who roamed the countryside scaring the wits out of passengers, but to astute promoters of flying circuses who realized that the stuntmen were only up there to attract attention. Once the yokels got to the airport, the job was to entice them into the sky for money.

119

Slats Rodgers used to be highly amused at the way his passengers worked up enough nerve to get off the ground for the first time: "Here would come some middle-aged wife traipsing behind her middle-aged husband, and they would fight anyone who wanted to horn in ahead of them, but they were scared to death all the time.

"About the time it was their turn, the man would want to back out. But the woman would argue him into it. Almost every time it was that way—the man was the one that had to be talked into going up. The woman did the talking."

Perhaps the one person who talked more people off the ground than anyone else was Ivan R. Gates, an old-time promoter of exhibition fliers before World War I, who originated the great Gates Flying Circus that air-lifted more than one million people between 1922 and 1928. Among Gates' early star performers had been Didier Masson, who later flew in the Mexican Revolution and with the Lafayette Escadrille in France, and Art Smith. The latter was a spectacular stunt flier who thrilled early air show audiences with pyrotechnic displays on night flights, during one of which he almost blew the tail off his pusher when his mechanic accidently tied giant firecrackers instead of flares to a strut.

Recognizing the great potential of aviation during the early postwar years, Gates teamed up with two West Coast barnstormers, Clyde Pangborn and Lowell Yerrex, and toured virtually every state in the nation. Lieutenant Pangborn, who had been a flight instructor at Ellington Field near Houston, Texas, was a careful pilot, and during his association with Gates hopped more than 125,000 passengers without a serious mishap.

Originators of the dollar ride, the Gates Flying Circus flew five-place Standards with Hisso engines and steel ladders bolted to their sides so passengers could be gotten in and out faster. One Gates pilot, Bill Brooks, broke all records by flying 980 passengers in a single day at Steubenville, Ohio! To do this, Brooks maintained a remarkable marathon schedule, taking off, circling the field and landing to empty his ship and take on a fresh load of passengers being herded through like cattle by the cigar-smoking Ivan Gates.

Passenger flying was big business to Gates, who paid his pilots up to $1,500 a month in order to get the best qualified men. It has been said that the

Gates Flying Circus turned out more famed pilots than the Army and Navy put together.

There was excitement too, along with the big push to get passengers airborne: there was the time a movie actress named Rosalie Gordon agreed to make a jump from Pangborn's ship with an old pull-out chute, but it got hung up in its container lashed between the wheels. Milton Girten, who was riding with them, clambered down to pull Rosalie back up, but the force of the wind was too much. Freddie Lund, also a wing-walker, swung over from another ship onto Pangborn's wing and crawled down to give Girten a hand. No luck. Both Girten and Lund were small men, agile but not muscular. So Lund, who was also a pilot, climbed back up and motioned Pang-

Airline pilot Harold Johnson flew with National Air Show on his days off. Here he loops a Ford Trimotor at ground level.

COURTESY ART INMAN

born to go help Girten while he flew the ship. That way they did get the poor girl back into the cockpit, and all four landed safely, making more headlines for the Gates Flying Circus, of course.

The first man to rig his Jenny for inverted flight, Pangborn once piloted it for a distance of two miles upside down, and after that he painted his name on the top wing. After the Gates Flying Circus broke up in 1928, Pangborn formed his own circus, the Flying Fleet, which came before he launched a new career as a world flier.

Almost as well-remembered as the Gates team of barnstormers was the Doug Davis Flying Circus, a group of deep-South gypsy pilots who banded together in 1924 when they realized their profits could soar if they put on a full-size air show instead of each doing a solo act. On their very first performance as a team, they took in $1,400 from the well-satisfied citizens of Opalaca, Alabama.

Davis, a wartime pilot trainee who came close to washing out a number of times at Kelly and Brooks Fields in Texas, started barnstorming in Atlanta, flying his clipped-wing Jenny from Chandler Race Track, today the site of one of the nation's busiest airports. When a competitor, Beeler Blevins, moved in, Davis moved out and began working the back country, where he introduced aviation to untold hundreds of country folk.

The Doug Davis Flying Circus stormed the countryside for a full year before running into fresh competition, this time in the form of a pretty Birmingham, Alabama, girl, Mabel Cody. Mabel was the first lass to risk

Doug Davis, head of Doug Davis Flying Circus, gets handshake from Vincent Bendix after winning 1934 Bendix Race.

her neck in a speedboat-to-plane change and was so well liked that she decided to organize her own show. This became the Mabel Cody Flying Circus, naturally, and it gave Doug Davis a headache. Whenever he led his squadron of war-surplus ships into a Southern town, it seemed that Mabel's troupe had already been there, skimming off the cream.

Mabel's pilots included a former Navy airman named Slim Culpepper and a wing-walker named Bonnie Rowe, who frequently had to put his parachute in hock. When it came time to put on his jump act, Bonnie would often have to sit up all night in a hotel room sewing bed sheets together for a makeshift canopy.

Curly Burns, Mabel Cody's promoter, was the first to see virtue (and profit) in billing the troupe's pilots as war heroes. Passengers paid more money to ride with this hero-star—whoever he happened to be on a particular day. So well did Mabel Cody's outfit do financially that Doug Davis flew over one day and tossed her a note in a bottle, suggesting that they bring the two shows together into one gigantic enterprise. Mabel turned him down cold. In addition, she began flying into towns Davis had already circularized, playing one-day stands to catch the bulk of his business.

There is the story of how the two flying circuses met one day over a small town and for a full hour fiercely battled each other all over the sky. True or not, there was intense rivalry until the Doug Davis show, adopting Mabel Cody's own tricks, began working itineraries she had already pitched with full page newspaper ads. Finally the two did join forces, and with a new sponsor, the Curtis Candy Company, were known henceforth as the Doug Davis Baby Ruth Flying Circus.

With the coming of the Depression years following the 1929 stock market collapse, the era of the gypsy flier drew to a close. Already, the Air Commerce Act of 1926 had shot down many of the baling-wire brigade of barnstormers who had not yet killed themselves in machines that couldn't come near passing an airworthiness inspection. It was a time for overhaul, for a new approach to country aviation, with some semblance of sanity in flying and licensing of plane and pilot to protect the public as well as the barnstormers themselves from needless tragedy.

Before we look at the new breed of barnstormer, the pilot in trim uniform who would give aviation a much-needed air of respectability, let's acknowledge one last time those old-bold heroes who soon would be flying west to vanish from the American scene.

There was Loxla Thornton, a heroic Alabamian who lost both arms in a railroad accident and yet barnstormed a Jenny with the aid of a steel forearm and hand and a versatile right shoulder. Strapped into a cockpit by his mechanic, he carried hundreds of passengers without accident until Department of Commerce inspectors grounded him. And there was Charles "Smiles" O'Timmons, a one-legged, one-armed parachutist remembered by aviation historian Russ Brinkley, who once got Smiles a job wing-walking in a show when the regular stunt man failed to show up. All went well until Smiles' artificial leg went through the Jenny's wing, fouling the control cables. In desperation, he pulled off his pants, unbuckled the leg and dove for the cockpit, to the great hilarity of the audience.

There was Major R. W. "Shorty" Schroeder, noted ex-Army pilot, who barnstormed a while before becoming chief pilot for Henry Ford and later a United Air Lines executive. And there was Lawrence Fritz, another World War I veteran who went broke barnstorming and became chief pilot for Bill Stout, designer of the Ford Trimotor "Tin Goose."

Colin "Boots" LeBoutillier, who never used his given first name, Oliver, went into barnstorming as a Royal Air Force hero who had helped to shoot down the famed Red Baron, Manfred von Richthofen. After the war he then drifted west to Hollywood to become an early member of the wild bunch known as the Motion Picture Pilots Association. Boots flew with Paul Mantz and Frank Clarke as wingman with the famed Hollywood Trio stunt team, which etched graceful patterns across the sky with special red, white and blue smoke LeBoutillier had invented. Others to join the MPPA ranks from the barnstorming circuit, besides Clarke, included Frank Tomick, a wartime March Field flight instructor, Ira Reed, an ex-Navy pilot, and "Colonel" Roscoe Turner, who won his commission as personal pilot of California's Governor "Sunny Jim" Rolph.

Colonel Turner, one of aviation's most colorful figures, was among the first to recognize the value of a natty uniform to impress customers, particularly the ladies. Resplendent in red jacket, green whipcord breeches, riding boots and waxed mustache, Turner looked exactly the way folks thought a pilot should look. He flew the way they liked, too, well enough to win the Bendix Trophy twice and set a number of city-to-city speed records nobody has gotten around to challenging.

Turner first went into barnstorming on borrowed money and with the rank of Lieutenant in the Air Service, and from the start knew how to please the crowds well enough to earn as much as $1,000 a day performing such spectacular stunts as "Falling a Mile in Flames"—a vertical dive performed with a smokepot. Teaming up with another barnstormer named Arthur H. Starnes, Turner formed the Roscoe Turner Flying Circus, which guaranteed to perform:

ONE WING-WALKING SHOW, INCLUDING THE
"SWING OF DEATH"
A PARACHUTE JUMP
AN AEROPLANE ACROBATIC FLIGHT, LOOPS, SPINS,
WINGOVERS, WHIP STALLS, ROLLS

Later on, Roscoe bought an eighteen-passenger Sikorsky, the first built in America, and for several years made broadcasts from the sky, staged aerial pink teas for society women and carried charter parties wherever they wanted to go. In Hollywood, Turner leased his Sikorsky to moviemaker Howard Hughes, who had it painted to resemble a German Gotha bomber for the great war film, *Hell's Angels*. If you saw the picture, maybe you remember

Colonel Roscoe Turner wore fancy uniforms with wings on chest, sleeves, collar, belt. He was a top racing pilot.

Will Rogers (left), the great humorist, was favorite of barnstormers like Tex Rankin.

the thrilling scene in which the Gotha, trailing smoke, spins to earth and crashes. Al Wilson, the pilot, found himself in a real, not a make-believe crisis when he heard a wing spar snap. He bailed out and lived, but a prop man named Phil Jones, operating the smokepot in the rear of the craft, failed to jump and was killed.

Other barnstormers went on to become aircraft company executives: Carl Squier was the first president of the Lockheed Aircraft Company; Alan Loughead, the founder of Lockheed when it was a small Santa Barbara, California, firm; and Tubal Claude Ryan, founder of the Ryan Aeronautical Company, who used one of Donald Douglas' Cloudsters to fly beer across the border from Mexicali to San Diego.

Enterprising Cliff Henderson, who staged the famous Cleveland National Air Races in the 1930's, bought three brand-new JN-4Ds in their crates, traded one to barnstormer Fred Kelly in return for a short course in flying and used the others to hop passengers who had been guaranteed a free ride with every car they bought from Henderson's Nash agency, a sideline business.

Wiley Post, another great barnstormer, started out as an oil-field roughneck in Oklahoma. He was bitten by the aviation bug when a flying circus hit Wewoka one day in 1919. When the regular parachute jumper broke his leg, Wiley volunteered to take his place for $50, leaping into space from the wing of a Canuck flown by Berl Tibbs. For a while Wiley became an airport tramp, following the barnstormers on their circuits, but when a gusher touched off a boom at Seminole, Oklahoma, he returned to the oil field. There something happened to change his life—the first day on the job, a splinter of steel blinded him in one eye.

Ironically, that accident got him back into flying, for with the $1,800 insurance money he bought a wheezing old Canuck and hired a flier named Sam Bartel to teach him to fly it. Wearing a black eyepatch and a leather helmet, Wiley Post was launched on a barnstorming career that would bring him world fame as a high-altitude flier, around-the-world pilot and finally as the man who met death with Will Rogers in a plane crash in Alaska.

One of the last, but not the least colorful, of this army of loners in the sky was Lieutenant Ralph Vaughn, who was one of Arizona's first two barnstormers. Vaughn and Charlie Mayse had discovered an untapped resource—the Apache Indians *loved* flying and would give the beads and silver trinkets off their backs to go up for a visit to Rain God country.

At first Vaughn operated with a Kreutzer K-3, which he had bought to set up an air link between Phoenix and Globe, a town in Apache territory. To drum up business, Vaughn sometimes took along a pair of wing-walkers and parachute jumpers, Suicide Slim and Reckless Rosie. In the 1930's, Vaughn bought a highwing Stinson R monoplane and until his retirement worked the Indian country throughout Arizona, Colorado, New Mexico and Utah with great success.

One by one, death thinned the ranks of the remaining independent barnstormers, who toward the end of the Roaring Twenties were finding the skies too crowded with competition or, in order to keep eating, tempted fate just once too often. There was Second Lieutenant Ormer Lester Locklear, a World War I flight instructor at Barron Field, Texas, who one day in luckier times was flying along with a student when his radiator cap blew off. Casually, Locklear clambered up on top of the Jenny's center section and stuck a rag in the hole to keep the scalding water from blowing back into the cockpits.

127

These twelve shots show the great Ormer Locklear at work. A former Air Corps instructor, Lieutenant Locklear was a nerveless wingwalker. He finally lost his life in film stunt plane crash.

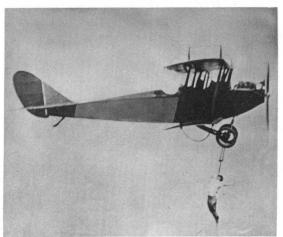

Other Army instructors at Barron heard about this and soon were trying to outdo each other with wing-walking stunts that petrified their students. Finally Locklear and two other mentors, Lieutenant Milton "Skeets" Elliot and Lieutenant Shirley Short, formed an exhibition team and went barnstorming, following Locklear's honorable discharge on May 5, 1919.

In January of that year, Locklear had made the first public plane change from one moving craft to another, over Love Field, Dallas. He then drifted west to become one of the madcap motion-picture pilots and stuntmen, until his death on August 2, 1920. Locklear was flying, with Skeets as a passenger, for a big scene for the movie *The Skywayman* that called for a night tailspin over Cecil B. DeMille Field, which was surrounded by blazing searchlights. Frank Clarke, who was there, remembered: "The cameras caught the silver wings as they twisted groundward. It was a beautiful scene, a dramatic shot. It seemed as if Locklear were outdoing himself in daring. And then in one minute the make-believe of pictures changed to tragedy in reality. . . . The plane hit the ground with a roar and shattered to bits. The mangled bodies of Locklear and Elliot were taken from the twisted mass. The battery of lights had been too strong and had blinded Locklear."

The wreckage, of course, was snapped up by Arrigo Balboni, the flying junkman, who added it to his collection of plane carcasses on Riverside Drive in Los Angeles. Balboni, who was born in Renazzo, Italy, and who learned to fly with the United States Army Air Service, once barnstormed a Jenny all the way around South America, up the East Coast of the United States, and finally into Alaska, before settling down. By the 1940's, with a new crop of Air Force pilots cracking up ships, Arrigo opened a bigger airplane junkyard closer to March Field, at a desert location he named Balboni, California (population 1).

Curiously, although perhaps one-tenth of America's population of a hundred million in the 1920's was introduced to flying by barnstormers (some esti-

Dale Seitz' Safe and Sane Flyers barnstorming troupe brought aviation to grassroots communities in Midwest.

COURTESY DALE SEITZ

LAST CHANCE
For
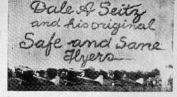

Dale A Seitz and his original Safe and Sane Flyers

(LOOK FOR THESE ORANGE PLANES)

AIRPLANE RIDES

——WITH——

LONG RIDE		Long High Ride
$2.50	**DALE A. SEITZ** AND HIS ORIGINAL	**$5.00**
See Your City From the Air	**SAFE AND SANE FLYERS**	Enables You to See Entire City

Friday, Saturday, Sunday
United States Government Licensed Planes and Pilots

FLYING FIELD ON WEST DIVISION STREET
——————AT BELLEVILLE——————

NO STUNT FLYING WITH PASSENGERS

With handbills and newspaper advertisements, the Safe and Sane Flyers circularized towns, luring crowds to the performing fields.

mates run to twenty per cent)—a far better record than the jet airlines can claim today, as a matter of fact—people were slow to accept scheduled flying, in the latter part of that hell-for-leather decade, as anything but a blue-sky dream. In 1926, a reporter for the Pekin, Illinois, *Daily Times* interviewed Dale Seitz, a barnstormer whose Safe and Sane Flyers troupe was operating in a field at the edge of town, near the Quaker Oats plant, and was told: "The time is rapidly approaching when any city that wishes to hold its own must have a municipal airport." Flying, Seitz assured the readers, "is a great experience, unlike anything else in the world. It does not make one dizzy, like standing on a tall building; rather, it affords a view of the city, rivers, lakes and fields that far surpasses the best maps ever made."

The next year, Seitz's Safe and Sane Flyers were cashing in on the Lindbergh boom, advertising, "Lindy crossed the ocean! You can see South Bend and your home from the air—enjoy a safe AIRPLANE RIDE!"

The Safe and Sane Flyers, who flew Wacos, Standards and other early OX-powered biplanes, naturally had their own stunt people, like "Daredevil Joe" LeBoeuf of Kankakee, Illinois, billed as "the world's oldest parachute

131

Pilots Bert Brown and Ted Fordon organized successful National Air Show, adopted fancy military uniforms, hired best-known pilots on barnstorming circuit.

jumper" who had been "diving out of airplanes and balloons for thirty-three years."

Dale Seitz' emphasis on flying safety was an indication of changing times. The image of the heroic gypsy flier was passé, and in his place was the crisp, efficient airman, a man you could trust. One of the first flying circuses to adopt this new image was the Fordon-Brown National Air Show, which boasted it was the only troupe of fliers to hold a Class One Bureau of Air Commerce waiver and $100,000 liability insurance with a property damage clause, in the event one of their pilots flew into the grandstand or hit a barn.

Created by two fliers named Bert Brown and T. N. Fordon, the National Air Show scouted the countryside for the most popular stunt fliers, hiring men like Milo Burcham, Dick Granere, Harold Johnson, Joe Jacobson, C. W. "Flash" Whittenbeck and Buddy Batzell, a parachute jumper. "The management," they announced, "has its fliers measured for special uniforms. The appearance of these ace fliers is neat. British-type uniforms set off with Sam Brown belts sound the death-knell of the oil-spattered, overalled fly-by-night aerial exhibitionists of the postwar barnstorming days. This is a new era in aeronautical entertainment."

"At the sound of an exploding bomb," they advertised, "a band strikes up a military air, leading the parade past the reviewing stand. Mounted state troopers add color and dignity to the occasion. Directly behind the band

132

marches the troupe of world-famous fliers which is the Fordon-Brown National Air Show. The band swings into the National Anthem, a bomb bursts overhead, a flag floats slowly to earth. And as the music fades away, another bomb explodes, an airplane roars down the field and surges aloft, and the show is on!"

And what a show! Instead of OX-Jennies, there was Flash Whittenbeck plunging through outside loops in a Great Lakes biplane, Milo Burcham snapping inverted in his Boeing P-12 fighter (how Burcham got it for civilian use he won't tell) and Joe Jacobson acrobating in his little white Howard racer (he takes it up to seven thousand feet and dives at the earth, engine wide open; down he comes at close to four hundred miles an hour, and then a few feet above the grass Joe pulls out in a screaming zoom!).

The finale was Buddy Batzell's grand parachute drop from the dizzying height of fourteen thousand feet: "After the first excited cry of recognition the crowd is deadly quiet. His body picks up speed, to 140 mph. Twelve thousand, ten, eight, six, four, two—will he *never* open his chute? Still he falls. Then there's a sharp crack! At that low altitude you can hear his twenty-eight-foot silken canopy whip open. He has fallen two miles in practically nothing flat. The show is over."

Not all barnstormers of the 1930's were out after speed records and passenger dollars. On September 14, 1933, a West Coast pilot, F. Myrten (Iron Hat) Johnston, won the dubious distinction of official recognition by the National Aeronautic Association for the nation's slowest plane flight: he averaged 37.008 mph over a 98-kilometer course in an Aeronca "flying bathtub" fitted with floats.

Johnston was an air show favorite with his skilled handkerchief pickup with a wingtip, takeoffs from the top of a touring car and endurance flights in which he grabbed five-gallon cans of fuel from an aide in a speedboat or automobile.

And then, finally, came the barnstorming transports—big, three-engine Ford "Tin Gooses," Fokkers, and Boeing Trimotors. People by the thousands began taking to the air, not to go somewhere but to get off the ground, up into the sky, just to ride around and look at the beauty of the country spread out below and realize they were in on the start of something marvelous, a

Iron Hat Johnston picks up handkerchief with wingtip of Aeronca Flying Bathtub.

revolution that some day would make air travel as safe and convenient as riding a train—and faster!

Brigadier General Leslie G. Mulzer, an airman who spent three years with the Strategic Air Command and served as 15th Air Force Commander at Colorado Springs, home of the Air Force Academy, was among those who came up from Jennies to Wacos and finally to Ford and Stinson Trimotors, as part of a glorious career "flying anything that would fly."

Howard Fisher Maish, holder of Transport Pilot License No. 68, was another ex-World War I barnstormer who graduated to Ford 4-ATs in 1930, barnstorming 175,000 miles across the United States, Canada, and Mexico for two years, making people airliner conscious.

One of the last to add glamour to barnstorming in the Trimotor era was Ben Gregory of Kansas City, who rigged his three-engine Ford transport with giant searchlights and with neon tubes outlining its great tin wings. This beast he called the *Ship from Mars,* and as he looped and rolled it through the sky, he pulled a lever that squirted kerosene into the exhaust stacks. Despite the shock of seeing huge flames and smoke plumes trailing from the engines, an estimated six hundred thousand people took a chance and went up to see what airline flying was like.

The greatest of the multi-engine barnstormers by far were the brothers Rolly, Don and Art Inman, whose Inman Brothers Flying Circus introduced a whole generation of Midwesterners to the glory of whistling across the sky in "America's largest Trimotor, the 80-A Boeing Clipper." It was Art Inman, in fact, who first came up with the name "Boeing Clipper" and who was obliged to sue the plane company for the right to retain it after they adopted it for their big flying boats that pioneered the Pacific Ocean runs.

More than one innocent would-be airline passenger made the mistake of climbing aboard the Inman Clipper, belting himself into one of the wicker seats and asking, "What time do we get to Chicago?" Art, resplendent in military uniform and silver wings, smiled and explained that it was only a local hop.

A confirmed realist, Art Inman more recently remembered with a laugh that the whole philosophy of barnstorming at the end of the 1920's and in the 1930's was aimed at building public confidence and used the tactic of making a farce of danger. "All rides are guaranteed to get you back in one piece!" Inman's barkers told the crowds. "Your money back if you get killed!"

Being a pilot was only a small part of what it took to be a barnstormer in those days, according to Art. "He had to be a politician, ballyhoo artist, con man, roustabout mechanic, showman, fence-mender and, of course be able to get a ship off the ground and back in one piece."

The Inman Brothers came along at a time when, strangely enough, local airport operators who should have welcomed the big business they drew either ordered them off the field or made them sign excessive thirty-day leases they couldn't afford. When the powers-that-be at Des Moines Municipal

Iron Hat Johnston tries fuel pickup from speeding car.

COURTESY IRON HAT JOHNSON

Don Inman died in this 1935 plane crash in Florida.   COURTESY ART INMAN

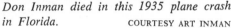

A boy and his kite that grew up. In 1918, Art Inman built and flew box kite, an early step in the airman's career.

Airport pulled that stunt on Art, they chose the wrong man. One night Art flew over the field with his 80-A Boeing Trimotor idling, then aimed the monster straight down, engines screaming and landing lights stabbing the sky. It was right after the Orson Welles "Martian Invasion" broadcast scare, and the Iowans were certain an L.G.M. (Little Green Man) was at the controls.

Inman had already arranged with city officials to provide a motorcycle escort for a giant portable searchlight he and his brother Rolley had rigged up. The airport officials were outraged, but the Inman Brothers Flying Circus did a land-office business that wouldn't stop.

Art, Rolley and Don Inman were not the last of the first barnstormers, but the first of the last. Rolley learned to fly under the tutelage of the great Speed Holman and was something of a master at the controls of their first barnstorming plane, a Lincoln Standard biplane. Luckily for his passengers, Rolley's skill once paid off when Art, landing with a good payload at Newton, Iowa, noted with a shock that the right wheel of Rolley's LS-5 had spun off just as he left the ground. Thinking fast, Art grabbed a loudspeaker and ordered everyone out onto the field. At the end of his hop, Rolley went furiously beet-red when he saw the rubes jamming his landing place, then paled, understanding the reason, when a mechanic held up the wheel. Rolley flew around until the crowd cleared off and then made a perfect one-wheel landing.

Another time early in the Inmans' career on a night flight from Waterloo, Iowa, a town well-named, he considered later, it was Art who faced disaster.

His Stinton Trimotor, loaded with paying passengers, pierced a sudden line squall fraught with turbulence that came close to ripping the wings off. When he finally found the field, only the baleful glare of auto headlights marked the runway instead of the powerful searchlight that was invariably lugged from town to town. Angrily confronting their assistant, Clifford Pitts, to demand an explanation of why he hadn't turned on the big beam, Clifford shrugged and spat. "You told me, Art, always cover it with the tarp if it rains, no matter what."

Well, there were good days and there were bad days in barnstorming, Art recalls. There were gay times they had with Kitty, a toothless old lion who weighed nine hundred pounds and who wrestled impressively with Art's wife as part of their circus routine, and there was the sheer joy of flying, taking up passengers and showing them what it was all about.

Sometimes Art was hard put to outwit the freeloaders who parked their Model T Fords outside the field and watched the air show for nothing. At such times he had a helper start a fire out on the field and set off a dynamite charge. A few moments later one of his brothers arrived on the scene, driving an ambulance, its siren screaming. The rubes then flocked through the gates like lemmings, to find out what had happened.

Rolley came close to death once when he flew the Ford Trimotor inverted, causing battery acid to spatter all over him. His bushy eyebrows kept him from being blinded, but he "put on the greatest acrobatic show of his life, jumping around the cockpit," Art remembers. That happened at Wichita,

Kitty, pet lion, poses with Inman Brothers Flying Circus troupe.

COURTESY ART INMAN

Rolley Inman, brother of Art, barnstormed until World War II. He was killed in 1944 plane crash.

Kansas, a town hostile to outside barnstormers and one where Inman found another way to break the monopoly on the local airport. He ran full-page ads in the newspapers, creating such a controversy that everybody in town came out to see what kind of a nut he was.

For all their frolicking, the Inman Brothers are remembered today for the expert and efficient way they went about their business. They dressed in neat, well-pressed uniforms and flew with such skill that some six hundred thousand Midwesterners were lured into the sky.

Death finally caught up with Don Inman, ironically as a passenger in another barnstormer's ship, on February 10, 1935, just four days after he had been grounded by the Department of Commerce (for not wearing a chute when he took up Carl Hall, the circus parachutist, for a jump). Rolley was killed nine years later, on June 19, 1944, in Maine, when a military C-54 transport he was ferrying on an Atlantic crossing hit a mountain peak during a rainstorm. Art, who was flying another ship ahead of him, had been shocked to hear Rolley get an incorrect weather briefing by radio. "He never had a chance," Art says sadly.

Art Inman, the sole survivor of the Inman Brothers Flying Circus, remembers that only World War II ended barnstorming, although today you'll

Inman Brothers Flying Circus had its own portable searchlight for night shows. Once, in 1938, they used it to help firemen put out fire in Centerville, Iowa. Inmans did such things to help break down opposition to itinerant flyers.

Ray Dugan, Inman Brothers Flying Circus mechanic, to help bring out the crowds, doubled as wing-walker.
COURTESY ART INMAN

Inman Brothers Flying Circus' Ford Trimotor over Wichita.

find a few stray pilots out beating the bushes for passengers on weekends. The author of this book remembers helping out a friend, Alvin Algee, who flew weekend passengers from a small airport in Compton, California, right after the war. One of the passengers was a little old lady who settled down in the back seat of Algee's Aeronca.

"Don't be scared when we lift off the ground," I reassured her. "Just relax and enjoy it."

At five hundred feet altitude, climbing over a highway, I glanced down and saw a convoy of military trucks inching along, bumper to bumper. There was a sudden, startling noise behind me, not unlike the chatter of a machine gun. I glanced around in alarm. The little old lady, her finger cocked, yelled, "Got every damn one of 'em!"

Art Inman, incidentally, became something of a World War II hero when, on July 1, 1941, he ferried the first Lockheed Lodestar across the Atlantic Ocean from the United States to British West Africa to spearhead the gigantic flow of lend-lease planes that helped divert the Nazi thrust into Africa. Today he lives not far from bustling Los Angeles International Airport, the thunder of jets a constant reminder of the barnstorming days when he helped America to grow wings.

Stop by at any airport today and you'll likely find some old-timers around, anxious to swap tales about the good old days of barnstorming, whether in the United States, Mexico or Canada. Bob Arabsky, an up-and-coming young bush pilot living in Winnipeg, Manitoba, reports the story of a charter pilot who was hopping passengers back into moose country, along with a case

139

Interior of Ford Trimotor was the ultimate in flying luxury: it had seats.

In the late 1930's the Inman Brothers airlifted more than half a million people in big Boeing Clipper and Ford Trimotor transports, introducing them to airline-type travel.

of Scotch. While waiting for a storm to pass, they opened a bottle. By the time the weather cleared they all fell into the aircraft, the pilot fumbling for the starter. One of his passengers got out to pull the blade through by hand just as the pilot hit the switch. But someone had forgotten to remove the canvas engine cover, and suddenly the guy outside found himself being whipped by lashing ropes. It sobered them all up pretty quickly.

Speaking of Canada, it was back in 1932 that a former Royal Air Force pilot named Wilfred Reid "Wop" May helped out the red-coated Royal Canadian Mounted Police in tracking down a fugitive known as the "mad trapper of Rat River."

The mad trapper, a man named Albert Johnson, led the Mounties on a twenty-nine day chase over the frozen Arctic wasteland. He was wanted for robbing Indian fur traps along the Rat, and, in an arrest attempt, shooting a constable in the chest. During the month-long manhunt, Johnson shot and killed a Mountie, then took off his snowshoes and disguised his tracks through the snow by combining them with those of a migrating moose herd.

The Redcoats finally appealed to "Wop" May, who went out looking for him in a ski-equipped Bellanca, which was armed with tear gas bombs, dynamite and 30-30 ammunition. Flying more than a thousand miles over the frozen tundra, the Canadian barnstormer finally picked up Johnson's trail near the Eskimo village of Aklavik, where a posse flushed him out and shot him. The dead trapper was found to have a grisly bag of gold teeth in his possession, plus $2,000 in cash.

The girls, lest we forget them, played their part in the barnstorming days when flying was a glorious adventure, and one should not overlook the cool, steady birdwomen—chicks, if you prefer—who added glamour to the skyways. Today's Powder Puff Derby had its origins in the barnstorming era, when the nation's top ladybirds competed in the First National Women's Air Derby, Santa Monica to Cleveland, in 1929. There was Louise Thaden, Bobbie Trout, Patty Willis, Marvel Crosson, Blanche Noyes, Vera Walker, Amelia Earhart, Marjorie Crawford, Ruth Elder and Florence "Pancho" Barnes. Marvel Crosson was killed, but the others found their way to Cleveland, with Louise Thaden the winner.

Aviatrix Helen Richey in 1934 became the first female airline pilot in America when she flew the right seat of a Central Airlines Ford Trimotor from Washington to Detroit.

Gladys Ingle of Hollywood made hair-raising plane changes, flying with the famed Thirteen Black Cats for the newsreels, but perhaps the most daring of the ladies was a lovely teenager, Margie Hobbs, who today lives in Miami, Florida, and from that sunny city can look back on her stunt career as a barnstormer billed as "Ethel Dare, the Flying Witch."

Ethel Dare, the Flying Witch (Margie Hobbs), thrilled crowds in 1920's with ninety-five plane changes.

Margie was a familiar figure around the old Ashburn Field near Chicago, where she first got the yen to scamper out on the wing of a Jenny and swing herself up onto another ship flying overhead, the first woman to make a plane-to-plane change in mid-air. In all, she performed the dangerous feat ninety-five times, hoping to make it an even hundred, before the pilots, a superstitious lot, refused to take her up any more.

One of her pilots, George W. Parmley, today remembers the time their circus was playing the Illinois State Fair in Detroit in 1920: "There was another plane-changer on the bill who was to perform first, before Ethel Dare. His two pilots made several unsuccessful approaches and on the third try he managed to grasp the ladder and leave the lower plane. But his hold was insecure and he lost his grip and came hurtling to the ground, falling about six hundred feet, end over end.

"We all stood watching the tragedy, and decided that Margie should be excused from performing that day, but she would have none of it. So we took off and she put on one of the best performances of her career."

Parmley's flying partner in the act was a man named Elmer Partridge, whose career dated back to 1910. Says Parmley, "After we finished with show business he decided to build an airplane for himself and incorporate his own ideas. He built this plane in an old and very small barn in Homewood, Illinois, and to everyone's amazement it not only flew but flew very impressively."

With this unusual plane, which featured an enclosed cockpit, Partridge became one of the first barnstormers to try to make the final transition to airline flying. This was on June 7, 1926, when he attempted, in the midst of a raging thunderstorm, to pioneer the dangerous Chicago-Twin Cities Air Mail Route, CAM-9.

Four pilots had already crashed to their deaths, and eight planes had been demolished in 1920, the year the Post Office Department started mail service over the route as a feeder line to the newly established transcontinental airway system. The run was shut down until Congressional passage of the Kelly Bill, an act designed to stimulate the airmail service. Then it was awarded to a bearded earlybird named Charlie Dickinson, a man who made his fortune in the seed business and spent it on planes. It was Dickinson who helped the noted designer Matty Laird build his great racers, such as Jimmy Doolittle's *Super Solution*, in Wichita.

An inveterate flier, Dickinson looked not unlike Santa Claus whipping across the sky, his whiskers flying in the wind, and as historian Henry Ladd Smith once observed, "The resemblance did not stop there."

On that June day in 1926 when Dickinson began operations on CAM-9, his mail fleet consisted of Partridge's three homebuilt Laird biplanes with OX-5 motors, and a Laird Swallow. Partridge climbed into his enclosed cockpit, signaled to the mechanic to turn the prop, then taxied out onto the runway at the Minneapolis field. He gunned the engine, lifted the tail and chugged off into the blinding storm, disappearing from sight. Moments later his ship was seen spinning down from the clouds. In the crash Partridge was killed, his lovely plane destroyed.

Within three months, all of Dickinson's pilots quit and all but one of his ships were wrecked. In August, 1926, he gave notice he was through and turned over his operation to Colonel L. H. Brittin, an officer of the St. Paul Chamber of Commerce, who, when he could find no other takers, decided to run the hard-luck airline himself. The line was called Northwest Airways, and it goes down in the history of aviation as the first barnstorming airline, one that lives today as Northwest Airlines, one of the world's major air carrier systems.

Brittin, an ex-Army colonel who knew absolutely nothing about flying, decided at the outset to hire only ex-barnstormers, wing-walkers and parachute jumpers. "We started with the idea that men who had barnstormed their own planes for years, through winter and summer, in the northwest territory we planned to serve, were the best men to fly our ships in that same district," he explained. "We had nothing against Army-trained pilots—they are fine fellows and fine fliers—but we believed that the men who had learned to nurse Wright pushers through the air, patch up wartime Jennies with haywire and keep them going and care for their own property to keep it flying, had peculiar gifts that we might utilize."

For his first pilot, Colonel Brittin picked Speed Holman, who, like Lindbergh, had started out as a parachute jumper, barnstorming the farming country of Minnesota, Montana and the Dakotas. Others who helped get Northwest going were Homer Cole, Chad Smith and Walter Bullock. Bullock logged more than thirty thousand hours in the air from the time he learned to fly back in 1916 at the old Curtiss Flying School at Newport News, Virginia.

They're still around, many of those great old barnstormers, so don't underrate those fatherly airline captains with graying temples who sit in air-conditioned cockpits and flash you across the sky at better than 600 mph.

There's Walter Hunter of American Airlines, the boy who hung by his knees from a Standard biplane and dove into haystacks. There are Dick Rossi and Bob Prescott, of the Flying Tiger Line, who barnstormed the Orient and flew with the Chinese in Burma, before America entered World War II. And there are Clay Lacy of United and Mira Slovak of Continental, dedicated transport drivers who spend their weekends out in the boondocks, flying open-cockpit racing planes close to the good sweet earth where all fliers come from, and to which they must someday return.

FOR FURTHER READING

THE AIR DEVILS
Don Dwiggins
J. B. Lippincott Co., 1966

THE AMERICAN HERITAGE HISTORY OF FLIGHT
Alvin M. Josephy, Jr., Editor
American Heritage Publishing Co., 1962

BARNSTORMING
Martin Caidin
Duell, Sloan & Pearce, 1965

THE CHALLENGING SKIES
C. R. Roseberry
Doubleday & Co., Inc., 1966

HEROINES OF THE SKY
Jean Adams & Margaret Kimball
Doubleday, Doran & Co., 1942

ONCE TO EVERY PILOT
Captain Frank Hawks
Stackpole Sons, 1936

SKY STORMING YANKEE
Clara Studer
Stackpole Sons, 1937

THE WORLD IN THE AIR
Francis Trevelyan Miller
G. P. Putnam's Sons, 1930

INDEX

146

147

148

Trout, Bobbie, 141
Turner, Roscoe, 22, 42, 124–125

U

Under My Wings, 43
Unger, Ivan, 80, 88

V

Valentin, Leo, 91
Vaughn, Ralph, 127
Veil, Charles Herbert, 25–26
Villa, Pancho, 107

W

Wade, Bill, 44
Waggener, Dick, 85
Walker, Vera, 141
Wanamaker, Rodman, 20, 55
Waterman, Waldo, 93
Welles, Orson, 136
Wells, Curly, 99

West Indies Aerial Express, 43
Whiteface, Chief, 88–89
Whittenbeck, C. W., 132
Willard, William A. P., 8–9
Williams, Alford J., 71
Williamson, Bob, 110
Willis, Patty, 141
Wilson, Al, 126
Wings Over America, 38
Woolaroc, 80, 85
Wright, Orville, 53
Wright brothers, 1
Wright Exhibition Co., 2
Wyatt, Ben, 79

Y

Yerrex, Lowell, 120
Young, Jimmy, 99

Z

Zaldo, Rafael de, 51

A NOTE ABOUT THE AUTHOR

DON DWIGGINS' interest in aviation began when a barnstormer with "a waxed mustache and beautiful boots" took ten-year-old Don up in a Jenny. He has been a flying enthusiast ever since.

At college, Mr. Dwiggins studied journalism and in his spare time researched and wrote a history of American ballooning in the 1800's. In World War II, he enlisted in the Glider Corps and later switched to the RAF as a flight instructor for three years.

When peace came, he bought seventeen surplus planes to start a non-scheduled airline that carried movie crews and equipment to filming locations. But this venture never became profitable and Mr. Dwiggins went back to journalism, first as aviation editor of the *Los Angeles Daily News,* then of the *Los Angeles Mirror.* In recent years, he has been associated with the Walt Disney Studios and Los Angeles television studio KKTV. He is also the author of several notable books about various aspects of aviation, among them a biography of Paul Mantz, the famous Hollywood stunt flier.